THE ANGLICAN CHANT BOOK

NOVELLO PUBLISHING LIMITED

Order No: NOV 040023

PREFACE

The purpose of this book has been to gather into a single volume those anglican chants—until now dispersed among many different collections—that are considered by expert opinion to be both worthy compositions in themselves and suitable for general use in parish churches. Almost every chant book in existence has been examined, and many hundreds of different chants have been considered, the inclusion or rejection of each one depending upon the opinion of the majority, not of a small editorial committee, but of a large number of Church musicians, both professional and amateur.

Special care has been taken in the allocation of the chants to the psalms, and, wherever possible, long-established associations have been retained. Certain chants that are known or believed to have been specially composed for the psalms to which they are herein set, or to have been considered by their composers as particularly suitable for these psalms, are indicated by the letter (S) after the number of the chant.

The chants have been so arranged that, whether the psalms sung at any service are those of the Day or those recommended in the Table of Proper Psalms (1928), dissonant key-sequences will not be encountered, provided that, where alternative chants are given, the appropriate alternatives are selected. Similarly, one or other of the chants set to *Venite* on each left-hand page will suitably precede any chant on that or on the corresponding right-hand page.

For most of the Canticles, chants are recommended from the body of the book, and should be used in rotation. In order to avoid the possibility of the same chant inadvertently being used twice during one service, the lists include the numbers of the psalms to which these chants are set.

The verse or verses of a psalm which should be sung to the second half of a double chant are indicated above such chants as are concerned.

Refrains and doxologies may be observed by singing them in unison, and an optional direction to this effect has been placed beneath the appropriate chants.

A number of chants with a high melodic range have been transposed to a lower key. In each case, however, the original key has been indicated, so that, if local conditions permit, the chant may be sung in that key. (A high reciting-note alone has not always been considered sufficient justification for transposing a chant to a lower key.) In certain chants that have been transposed, alternative notes, an octave higher, have been inserted for the bass part.

Grateful acknowledgment is made to the following for permission to use their copyright chants :

Mr. E. W. Atkins, 180 ; Mrs. Brazier, 79, 82, 346 ; Sir Edward Bridges, 348, 375 ; Canon D. B. Eperson, 15 (76), 156 (238), 179 (278), 347 ; Mrs. Gouriet, 223 ; Mr. H. M. Havergal, 240 (360, 382) ; Miss E. Hodgson, 61, 323 ; Mr. F. Jackson, 70 ; The Provost and Fellows of King's College, Cambridge, and Dr. E. R. Goodlyffe, 100 (149) ; Dr. H. G. Ley, 182, 271 ; Miss D. Luard-Selby, 41 (250) ; Dr. C. H. Moody, 33 (71, 294, 337) ; Mr. W. J. Mothersole, 131 ; The Oxford University Press, 63, 77, 105 (237, 324), 154, 167, 195, 198, 205, 235, 263, 304, 307, 310, 328, 364, 371, 388 ; Miss B. M. Palmer, 113 (177) ; The Royal School of Church Music, 243 ; Mr. W. E. Smith, 369 ; Dr. G. T. Thalben-Ball, 241 ; Dr. F. W. Wadely, 203, 229 ; Mr. J. Wilson, 173, 327.

The copyright of the following chants is owned by Messrs. Novello and Co. :

4 (386), 34, 52, 69, 72 (353), 159, 183, 209, 210, 211, 214, 343, 359, 362, 384, 387, 390.

The following have taken part in the production of this book :

PRESENT AND PAST CATHEDRAL ORGANISTS

Doctors R. J. Ashfield (Southwell), J. Dykes Bower (Truro, Durham, and St. Paul's), A. V. Butcher (Llandaff), R. H. P. Coleman (Peterborough), M. P. Conway (Chichester and Ely), E. T. Cook (Southwark), H. Goss Custard (Liverpool), R. Head (Edinburgh), H. G. Ley (Christ Church, Oxford, and Precentor of Eton), H. S. Middleton (Truro, Ely, and Trinity College, Cambridge), J. R. Middleton (Chelmsford and Chester), C. H. Moody (Ripon), P. G. Saunders (Wakefield), H. D. Statham (Norwich), H. C. L. Stocks (St. Asaph) ; Messrs. C. P. P. Burton (St. Alban's), E. A. Coningsby (Llandaff,) A. Meredith Davies (St. Alban's and Hereford), T. L. Duerden (Blackburn), C. W. Eden (Durham), E. P. Hallam (St. Edmundsbury), C. Harker (Bristol), H. A. Hawkins (Chichester), F. Jackson (York), G. H. Knight (Canterbury, and Director of the Royal School of Church Music), K. F. Malcolmson (Newcastle), F. G. Ormond (Truro), A. P. Porter (Lichfield), R. A. Surplice (Bristol and Winchester), W. S. Vann (Chelmsford and Peterborough), D. V. Willcocks (Salisbury and Worcester), together with Sir William McKie (Westminster Abbey), Doctors E. S. Roper (Chapels Royal) and A. M. Cook (Leeds Parish Church), and Mr. R. Orr (St. John's College, Cambridge).

OTHER ORGANISTS AND CHURCH MUSICIANS

Messrs. L. J. Blake (Malvern College), J. Brough (St. Edmund's School, Canterbury), C. L. P. Hutchings (Wolverhampton Collegiate Church), S. W. G. Ives (St. Mary of Eton, Hackney Wick), J. V. Peters (Assistant, Southwell Minster), P. B. Tomblings (Merchant Taylors' School), J. C. Winter (Assistant, Truro Cathedral), E. J. Wright (Headquarters Choirmaster of the Royal School of Church Music) ; together with Lord St. Audries, Canon Lancelot Smith, the Misses L. M. Gordon and M. Walton (Music Librarian, Barber Institute of Fine Arts, Birmingham University), Messrs. W. L. L. Baker, D. J. Cox, H. Elliott, F. E. E. Harvey, M. Hawkins, A. J. Hayden, C. Holt, and many others.

PRESENT AND PAST MINOR CANONS

The Very Reverend N. T. Hopkins (St. Paul's and Provost of Wakefield), the Reverend Canon L. G Bark (Carlisle), Canon D. B. Eperson (Chichester), Canon R. T Lambert (St. Edmundsbury), Prebendary E. L. Millen (Wells), J. P. Boden (Winchester), J. H. A. Charles (Canterbury), V. Dams (Manchester), R. J. Edmondson (Carlisle), H. C. Robinson Eltoft (Manchester), A. J. Gill (Peterborough), J. B. Goodchild (St. Edmundsbury), J. L. Lawson (Hereford, Ely, and Canterbury), R. S. N. Lee (Carlisle, Truro, Gloucester, and Ely), G. Milroy (Exeter), F. H. J. Newton (St. Alban's), A. G. W. Paget (Peterborough and Norwich), C. K. Pattinson (Durham), H. E. Ruddy (Manchester), K. J. F. Skelton (Wells), H. Spence (York, and Clerical Commissioner of the Royal School of Church Music), Dr. F. Streatfeild (Christ Church, Oxford), J. E. F. Styles (Christ Church, Oxford), J. R. Thomas (Southwell), J. Webster (Truro), H. G. Welch (Rochester), P. W. Wigginton (Southwell),

together with the Compiler:

The Reverend R. E. Sibthorp (Peterborough and Truro)

and

Mr. H. A. Chambers (of Messrs. Novello and Co. Ltd.)

INDEX

Where a chant has been transposed, the original key is shown in brackets.

S — Single. D — Double. T — Triple. Q — Quadruple.

		Key	No.
Blow, John, D.Mus., Cantuar. 1648-1708. Organist of Westminster Abbey; Gentleman, Master of the Children, and Composer at the Chapel Royal. (The first recorded Lambeth D.Mus.)	S	E minor	373
Boyce, William, Mus.D., Cantab. 1710-79. Organist and Composer to the Chapel Royal.	D	D	60
Bridges, Mrs. Mary Monica. 1863-1949. Wife of Robert Bridges, Poet Laureate.	S	F	348
	D	A minor	375
Brown, A. (Identity uncertain. The chant occurs in the Wells Cathedral Chant Book.)	S	G(A♭)	251
Buck, Sir Percy Carter, D.Mus., Oxon. 1871-1947. Organist of Wells and Bristol Cathedrals; Director of Music, Harrow; Professor of Music, Dublin and London.	D	G	232
Burton, Robert Senior. 1820-92. Organist of Leeds Parish Church.	S	F	261, 338
Camidge, John, junr., Mus.D., Cantab. et Cantuar. 1790-1859. Organist of York Minster.	D	E	160
Camidge, Matthew. 1758-1844. Organist of York Minster; father of the above.	D	E♭, D	20, 123
	D	E minor	65, 197
(adapted by S. Elvey	D	E	66, 196
Carter, Rev. Edmund Sardinson. 1845-1923. Vicar Choral and Sub-Chanter of York Minster.	D	A♭	70
Champneys, Sir Frank Henry, 1st Bart., D.M., Oxon., F.R.C.P. 1848-1930. Physician at St. Bartholomew's Hospital.	S	F(G)	216, 302
Chipp, Edmund Thomas, Mus.D., Cantab. 1823-86. Organist of Ely Cathedral.	D	E	175
Clark, Richard. 1780-1856. Lay Clerk of St. George's, Windsor, and of Eton; Lay Vicar of Westminster Abbey; Vicar Choral of St. Paul's; Gentleman of the Chapel Royal.	D	A minor	370
Cobb, Gerard Francis. 1838-1904. Junior Bursar and Fellow of Trinity College, Cambridge; President of the University Board of Musical Studies.	S	E	134, 354
Cooke, Benjamin, Mus.D., Cantab. et Oxon. 1734-93. Organist of Westminster Abbey.	S	F	86, 234
Cooke, Robert. 1768-1814. Organist of Westminster Abbey; son of the above.	D	C minor	267
	D	F(G)	5, 381
	D	F(G)	11, 125
Cooper, George. 1820-76. Organist of the Chapel Royal.	D	G	181
Corfe, Dr. (Identity uncertain; apparently not C. W. Corfe.)	S	G	122, 341
Croft, William, D.Mus., Oxon. 1678-1727. Organist of Westminster Abbey.	S	A minor	103
Crotch, William, D.Mus., Oxon. 1775-1847. First Principal of the Royal Academy of Music	S	B♭	215
	D	A	51
	D	C	74
	D	F	137
	D	G	380

	Key	No.
CUTLER, EDWARD, Q.C. 1831-1916. Organist of Whitchurch, Edgware; Grand Organist to the Grand Lodge of Freemasons.	D F(G)	183
DAVIES, SIR WALFORD, Mus.D., Cantab. 1869-1941. Organist of the Temple Church and St. George's, Windsor; Master of the King's Musick.	S A minor	173
	S C(B) minor	327
DAVY, JOHN. 1763-1824. Composer of songs.	D D	7, 129
DIX, LEOPOLD LANCASTER. 1861-1935. A Dublin solicitor.	S A minor	198
	S F	364
	S G	63
DUPUIS, THOMAS SAUNDERS, D.Mus., Oxon. 1733-96. Organist and Composer to the Chapel Royal.	S A minor	138
	S D minor	332
	D A♭(A)	299
DYCE, WILLIAM, R.A. 1806-64. Eminent portrait painter; pioneer in reviving interest in Plainsong.	S F	285
EDWARDS, EDWIN, F.C.O. 1830-1907. Organist and Choirmaster of Rugby School.	D F	217
ELGAR, SIR EDWARD WILLIAM, 1st Bart., O.M., Mus.D., Cantab., Dunelm, Oxon., et Yale. 1857-1934. Master of the King's Musick.	S F(G)	72, 353
ELVEY, SIR GEORGE JOB, D. Mus., Oxon. 1816-93. Organist of St. George's, Windsor.	S B♭	133, 336, 366
	S B♭	383
	D C	270
	D D	165
	D D	308
	D E♭(F)	30
	D E	231
	D F	305
	D F	311
	D G(A♭)	8, 67
ELVEY, STEPHEN, D.Mus., Oxon. 1805-60. Organist of New College, Oxford, and Choragus of the University; brother of the above.	S B♭	121, 218
	D E	94
	D F	303
	D G	28, 309
EPERSON, REV. DONALD BIRKBY. 1904- Canon Emeritus of Salisbury; Chaplain of Bishop Otter College, Chichester.	S B♭	15, 76
	S D	156, 238
	S D	179, 278
	S D minor	347
FARRANT, RICHARD. d. 1580. Gentleman of the Chapel Royal; Lay Clerk, Master of the Choristers, and Organist of St. George's, Windsor.	S F	351
FELTON, REV. WILLIAM. 1713-69. Sub-Chanter of Hereford Cathedral.	S E♭	147
FLINTOFT, REV. LUKE. d. 1727. Minor Canon of Westminster Abbey. (It is probable that he was only the arranger of this chant, the melody of which can be traced in a psalm tune in *Allison's Psalter* (1599), and later, under the name "Salisbury", in John Playford's *Whole Booke of Psalms* (1677).)	D F(G) minor	46, 139
FOSTER, JOHN. 1827-1915. Organist of St. Andrew's, Wells Street; Lay Vicar of Westminster Abbey; Gentleman of the Chapel Royal.	D E	52

		Key	No.
Fox, J. M. (Identity uncertain.)	D	D♭	95
Frye, John Thomas. 1812-87. Organist of Saffron Walden Church from the age of eight until three years before his death.	S	E	287
Garrett, George Mursell, Mus.D., Cantab. 1834-97. Organist of St. John's College, Cambridge, and to the University.	S	D	200, 334
	D	F	162
	D	G	164
	D	G	330
Gibbons, Christopher, D.Mus., Oxon. 1615-76. Organist of Winchester Cathedral, the Chapel Royal, and Westminster Abbey.	S	G	207
Gladstone, Francis Edward, Mus.D., Cantab. 1845-1928. Organist of Llandaff, Chichester, and Norwich Cathedrals.	D	F	248
Goodson, Richard, B. Mus., Oxon. 1655-1718. Organist of New College and Christ Church, Oxford; Professor of Music in the University.	S	C	22, 87, 295, 349
Goss, Sir John, Mus. D., Cantab. 1800-80. Composer to the Chapel Royal; Organist of St. Paul's Cathedral.	S	A	99, 289, 350
	S	D minor	333
	D	A♭(B♭)	253
	D	A♭(A)	317
	D	B minor	202
	D	C minor	55
	D	C minor	142
	D	D	64
	D	E♭(F)	39
	D	E♭	146
	D	E♭	300
	D	E	106
(from J. Clarke)	D	F(F♯) minor	40, 143
	D	G(A)	171
Greene, Maurice. 1695-1755. Organist of St. Paul's Cathedral and the Chapel Royal.	S	A♭(B♭)	245, 313
Hanforth, Thomas William, Mus.B., Dunelm. 1867-1948. Organist of Sheffield Cathedral.	S	D	25, 301
Harrison, J. (Identity uncertain; probably either John Harrison, 1808-71, Organist of St. Andrew's, Deal, or John Harrison, Organist of St. Botolph's, Aldgate, 1867-80.)	S	D	26
Havergal, Henry MacLeod, B.Mus., Edin. 1902- Director of Music, Fettes College, Edinburgh, Haileybury, Harrow, and Winchester College; Principal of the Royal Scottish Academy of Music.	T	C	240, 360, 382
Havergal, Rev. William Henry. 1793-1870. Hon. Canon of Worcester; great-grandfather of the above.	S	E	90, 145
	D	E	107
Hayes, Philip, D.Mus., Oxon. 1738-97. Gentleman of the Chapel Royal; Organist of New College, Magdalen, and St. John's College, Oxford.	S	E minor	43
	S	E	44
Hayes, William, D.Mus., Oxon. 1707-77. Organist of Magdalen College, Oxford, and Professor of Music in the University; father of the above.	S	A	88
	S	A minor	89
	S	C(D)	242

		Key	No.
Heathcote, Rev. Gilbert. c.1770-1829. Amateur composer.	D	G(A)	319
Henley, Rev. Phocion. 1728-64. Rector of St. Andrew's-by-the-Wardrobe with St. Anne's, Blackfriars.	D	E♭	236
Higgins, Edward. d. 1769. Organist of Bristol Cathedral; Vicar Choral of Christ Church and St. Patrick's Cathedrals, Dublin.	D	E♭(F)	321
Hindle, John, B.Mus., Oxon. 1761-96. Lay Vicar of Westminster Abbey.	S	G	24, 144
Hodgson, Miss Ethel. Amateur composer of the twentieth century.	S	G	61
	D	D♭	323
Hopkins, Edward John, Mus.D., Cantuar. 1818-1901. Organist of the Temple Church for fifty-five-years.	S	E♭	83
	D	A♭	322
	D	C	29
	D	F	296
	D	F(G)	220 (224)
	D	F(G) minor	222
Hopkins, John Larkin, Mus.D., Cantab. 1820-73. Organist of Rochester Cathedral and Trinity College, Cambridge; cousin of the above.	S	C	12, 352
	D	C(D)	10, 258
Humfrey, Pelham. 1647-74. Gentleman, and Master of the Children, of the Chapel Royal.	S	C	389
Jones, John. 1728-96. Organist of St. Paul's Cathedral.	S	D	169, 260
	D	A	158
Keeton, Haydn, D.Mus., Oxon. 1847-1921. Organist of Peterborough Cathedral.	S	B♭	17, 340
Kelway, Thomas. c.1695-1749. Organist of Chichester Cathedral.	S	C(D)	49
	S	G minor	206
Knight, Gerald Hocken, Mus.B., Cantab. 1908- Organist of Canterbury Cathedral; Director of the Royal School of Church Music.	D	G(A♭)	243
Knyvett, William. 1779-1856. Gentleman of the Chapel Royal; Lay Vicar of Westminster Abbey. (from Handel)	D	F	38
Langdon, Richard, B.Mus., Oxon. 1729-1803. Organist of Exeter, Ely, Bristol, and Armagh Cathedrals.	D	F	135
Lawes, Henry. 1595-1662. Composer of Masques and Ayres. (Chant adapted by J. Corfe.)	D	B♭, C	13, 266
Lemon, John. 1754-1814. Lt.-Col. in the Army; Lord Commissioner of the Admiralty; M.P. for Truro and other Cornish boroughs; distinguished amateur musician.	D	D	255
	D	G	314
Ley, Henry George, D.Mus., Oxon. 1887- Organist of Christ Church, Oxford, and Choragus of the University; Precentor of Eton.	S	F	105, 237, 324
	D	A(B♭)	182
	D	B♭	205
	D	C	271
	D	C	328
	D	C minor	235
	D	D	154
	D	D	263
	D	E	388

		Key	No.
Lloyd, Charles Harford, D.Mus., Oxon. 1849-1919. Organist of Gloucester Cathedral and Christ Church, Oxford; Precentor of Eton; Organist and Composer to the Chapel Royal.	S	A	69
	S	G♭	362
	D	A♭(B♭)	359
Longhurst, William Henry, D.Mus., Cantuar. 1819-1904. Organist of Canterbury Cathedral.	D	B♭(C)	80
Luard-Selby, Bertram. 1853-1919. Organist of Salisbury and Rochester Cathedrals.	S	A♭(B♭)	41, 250
Luther, Martin. 1483-1546. (Chant adapted from the chorale, *Ein' feste Burg*.)	D	C	127
Macfarren, Sir George Alexander, D.Mus., Oxon. et Cantab. 1813-87. Professor of Music, Cambridge; Principal of the Royal Academy of Music.	S	A	47, 114, 189
	S	A minor	115, 176
	S	B♭(C)	85
	S	B♭	126
Mann, Arthur Henry, D.Mus., Oxon. 1850-1929. Organist of St. Peter's, Wolverhampton, Beverley Minster, and King's College, Cambridge.	D	A minor	100, 149
Marchant, Sir Stanley, C.V.O., D.Mus., Oxon. 1883-1949. Organist of St. Paul's Cathedral; Principal of the Royal Academy of Music; Professor of Music, London.	D	G♭	307
Marsh, William. 1757-1818. Lieut., R.N.; brother of John Marsh, Organist of Chichester Cathedral.	D	A	385
Martin, Sir George Clement, Mus.D., Cantuar. 1844-1916. Organist of St. Paul's Cathedral.	D	A♭	214
	D	A♭	343
	D	A	210
	D	F	34
Massey, Richard. 1798-1883. Organist of the Chapel Royal, Whitehall. (Or the composer may have been an earlier Richard Massey, probably the father of the above.)	D	A	281
Miller, Charles Edward. 1856-1933. A solicitor; Organist of St. Augustine's with St. Faith's, Watling Street, London, and Lambeth Parish Church.	D	B♭	310
	D	D	195
	D	E♭	77
Monk, Edwin George, D.Mus., Oxon. 1819-1900. Organist of York Minster.	S	A minor	31
	S	A	32, 178
	S	C(D)	37, 59, 108, 201, 367
	S	E minor	91
	S	F	249
	S	G	378
	D	G(A♭)	239
Monk, Walter. 1888-1914. Son of Dr. Mark James Monk, Organist of Truro Cathedral.	D	E	161
Moody, Charles Harry, Mus.D., Cantuar. 1874- Organist of Ripon Cathedral.	S	C	33, 71, 294, 337
Morley, William, B.Mus., Oxon. c.1680-1731. Gentleman of the Chapel Royal.	D	D minor	136
Mornington, Garrett Colley Wellesley, Earl of, Mus.D., Dublin. 1735-81. Professor of Music, Dublin; father of the Duke of Wellington.	D	D♭(D)	316

		Key	No.
Mothersole, Wilfred John. 1898- Assistant-Organist of St. Edmundsbury Cathedral.	D	G(A)	131
Nares, James, Mus.D., Cantab. 1715-83. Organist of York Minster and the Chapel Royal.	S	A	166
Naylor, John, D.Mus., Oxon. 1838-97. Organist of York Minster.	S	A minor	213
	T	F	27, 117, 193
Norris, Thomas, B.Mus., Oxon. 1741-90. Composer and tenor singer.	D	A	35
Novello, Vincent. 1781-1861. Organist of the Portuguese Chapel, South Street, Grosvenor Square, and the Roman Catholic Chapel, Moorfields; founder of the music-publishing firm of Novello and Co.	S	A	192
Oakeley, Sir Herbert Stanley, Mus.D., Cantuar., Oxon. et Dublin. 1830-1903. Professor of Music, Edinburgh.	Q	F	16
Ouseley, Rev. Sir Frederick Arthur Gore, Bart., LL.D., D.Mus., Oxon. et Cantab. 1825-89. Professor of Music, Oxford; founder of St. Michael's College, Tenbury.	S	C	45, 58, 290, 355, 377
	S	C(D)	233
	S	D	3, 116
	S	E	36
	S	F(G)	269, 335
	S	G	153, 274
	D	A♭	21
	D	A♭	97
	D	F	372
Palmer, Clement Charlton, D.Mus., Oxon. 1871-1944. Organist of Canterbury Cathedral.	S	D	113, 177
Parisian Tone.	S	E	50
Parratt, Sir Walter, Hon. D.Mus., Oxon. 1841-1924. Organist of St. George's, Windsor; Professor of Music, Oxford.	D	C	4, 386
	D	D	159
Prendergast, William, D.Mus., Oxon. 1868-1933. Organist of Winchester Cathedral.	D	F minor	223
Pye, Kellow John, B.Mus., Oxon. 1812-1901. Composer and pianist.	D	E♭	298
Randall, John, Mus.D., Cantab. 1715-99. Professor of Music in the University.	D	D	282
Rhodes, Harold William, Mus.D., Lond. 1889- Organist of Coventry and Winchester Cathedrals.	D	C	304
	D	E♭	371
Rimbault, Edward Francis, Hon. D.C.L., Oxon. 1816-76. Lecturer and writer on music; antiquarian.	S	A♭	140
	S	C minor	326
	S	F	118, 184, 225, 268
Robinson, John. 1682-1762. Organist of Westminster Abbey.	D	E♭	14, 56
Rogers, Sir John Leman, Bart. 1780-1847. Composer and amateur enthusiast.	D	E♭	344
Russell, William, B.Mus., Oxon. 1777-1813. Organist of the Foundling Hospital.	S	E♭	226, 312, 342
	S	G	112, 157
	D	C	221
	D	E♭(E)	315
	D	E	18

		Key	No.
Slater, Gordon Archbold. Mus.D., Dunelm. 1896- Organist of Leicester and Lincoln Cathedrals.	S	G	167
Smart, Henry. 1813-79. Organist of St. Pancras Church.	S	C(D)	280
	S	F	212, 291
	D	A minor	42, 275
	D	D	130
	D	D	256
	D	D minor	219
	D	G	2, 358
	D	G(A)	262
Smith, John Stafford. 1750-1836. Organist and Master of the Children of the Chapel Royal.	D	A♭	357
Smith, Walter Ernest, B.Mus., Oxon. 1879- Assistant Music Master, Clifton College.	D	C(C♯) minor	369
Soaper, John. 1743-94. Composer and singer.	D	D	186
South, Charles Frederick. 1850-1916. Organist of Salisbury Cathedral.	D	C	101, 151, 276
Stainer, Sir John, D.Mus., Oxon. 1840-1901. Organist of St. Paul's Cathedral.	S	C	6, 78
	S	G	259
(from Beethoven)	D	D	331
Stanford, Sir Charles Villiers, D.C.L., LL.D., Mus.D., Cantab. et Oxon. 1852-1924. Professor of Music, Cambridge.	S	C	390, 391
	D	A♭	387
	D	D minor	209
	D	E♭	384
Stephens. (Identity uncertain ; almost certainly not C. E. Stephens.)	S	A(B♭)	104, 168, 277
Stewart, Charles Hylton, Mus.B., Cantab. 1884-1932. Organist of Rochester and Chester Cathedrals, and St. George's, Windsor.	S	C(D)	79
	S	C minor	82
	S	C minor	346
Stonex, Henry. 1823-97. Assistant-Organist of Norwich Cathedral ; Organist of Great Yarmouth Parish Church.	D	F(F♯) minor	252
Tallis, Thomas. c.1520-85. Gentleman of the Chapel Royal.	S	B minor	363
Thalben-Ball, George Thomas, D.Mus., Cantuar. 1896- Organist of the Temple Church ; Musical Adviser to the Religious Broadcasting Department, B.B.C.	S	G	241
Tomkins, Thomas. 1573-1656. Organist of the Chapel Royal and Worcester Cathedral.	S	A♭	155
Tonus Peregrinus.	S	E minor	286
'Trent.' (This chant was composed by Sydney Bevan, 1838-1901, and named after his home, Trent Park, Middlesex.)	D	A♭	230
Tucker, Rev. William. c.1630-79. Precentor of Westminster Abbey.	S	A	246
Turle, James. 1802-82. Organist of Westminster Abbey.	S	E♭	293
	S	E	68
	S	G	284
	D	A♭(A)	54
	D	A♭(A)	329
	D	C	96
	D	C(D) minor	110

		Key	No.
Turle, James, (*contd.*)	D	D♭	120
	D	D minor	187
	D	D	188
	D	F	53
	D	F	92
	D	F	339
(from H. Purcell)	D	F minor	345
	D	G	128
(from J. S. Bach)	D	G(A) minor	376
Turton, Right Rev. Thomas, D.D. 1780-1864. Dean of Peterborough and Westminster; Regius Professor of Divinity, Cantab.; Bishop of Ely.	S	F(G)	48, 247
Wadely, Frederick William, Mus.D., Cantab. 1882- Organist of Carlisle Cathedral.	D	C minor	203
	D	F minor	229
Walmisley, Thomas Attwood, Mus.D., Cantab. 1814-56. Professor of Music in the University.	S	D	279, 325
	D	A, A♭	19, 265
	D	C	163
	D	D	191
	D	E♭	318
	D	F	132
Wesley, Samuel. 1766-1837. Son of Charles, and nephew of John, Wesley.	D	E♭(F)	254
	D	F(A) minor	93
	D	G	119
Wesley, Samuel Sebastian, D.Mus., Oxon. 1810-76. Organist of Hereford and Exeter Cathedrals, Leeds Parish Church, and Winchester and Gloucester Cathedrals; son of the above.	S	D minor	208
	S	E minor	152
	D	D minor	194
	D	F	75
Wickes, Rev. Croome Allan. c.1824-60. Curate of Holdenby, and St. Andrew's, Marylebone.	S	C(D) minor	374
Woodward, Richard, Mus.D., Dublin. 1744-77. Organist of Christ Church Cathedral, Dublin.	D	D	1, 170
	D	G(A)	297

LIST OF CHANTS FOR THE CANTICLES

EASTER ANTHEMS

(and Jubilate Deo)

Chants 118, 246, 247, or any chant appointed for *Venite*.

BENEDICTUS

Chant	Chant	Chant
28 (Ps. 3)	107 (Ps. 37)	300 (Ps. 119 v. 25)
29 (Ps. 4)	119 (Pss. 42 and 43)	303 (Ps. 119 v. 33)
66 (Pss. 22 and 78)	135 (Ps. 50)	308 (Ps. 119 v. 73)
80 (Ps. 27)	154 (Ps. 61)	314 (Ps. 119 v. 105)
92 (Ps. 31)	175 (Ps. 69)	316 (Ps. 119 v. 121)
94 (Ps. 32)	186 (Ps. 73)	321 (Ps. 119 v. 153)
97 (Ps. 34)	283 (Ps. 112)	371 (Ps. 141)
102 (Pss. 35 and 119 v. 57)	292 (Ps. 116)	379 (Ps. 144)
	298 (Ps. 119 v. 9)	

MAGNIFICAT

(and Cantate Domino)

Note.—The key of the Chant should be related to that of the Office Hymn, when one is used.

Key	Chant	Key	Chant
A♭	54 (Ps. 18)	E♭	236 (Ps. 94)
	253 (Ps. 102)		254 (Ps. 103)
	357 (Ps. 135)		315 (Ps. 119 v. 113)
	387 (Ps. 149)	E	388 (Ps. 149)
A	51 (Ps. 16)	F	38 (Ps. 9)
	385 (Ps. 147)		220 (Ps. 89)
C	101 (Pss. 35, 59 and 109)		296 (Ps. 118)
D♭	95 (Ps. 32)	G	128 (Ps. 47)
D	60 (Ps. 19)		171 (Ps. 68)
	64 (Ps. 21)		232 (Ps. 92)
	165 (Ps. 66)		239 (Ps. 96)
	263 (Ps. 105)		243 (Ps. 98)
	282 (Ps. 111)		380 (Ps. 145)

NUNC DIMITTIS

(and Deus Misereatur)

Chant	Chant	Chant
49 (Ps. 15)	126 (Ps. 45)	286 (Ps. 114)
50 (Ps. 15)	166 (Ps. 67)	348 (Ps. 131)
62 (Ps. 20)	167 (Ps. 67)	351 (Ps. 132)
68 (Ps. 23)	249 (Ps. 101)	364 (Ps. 138)

TE DEUM LAUDAMUS

FIRST SET

1 (also for Psalms 41, 68 and 135) R. Woodward

2 Thou art the King of glory. H. Smart

3 O Lord, save thy people. F. A. G. Ouseley

SECOND SET

4 (also for Psalms 27, 145 and 148) W. Parratt

5 Thou art the King of glory. R. Cooke

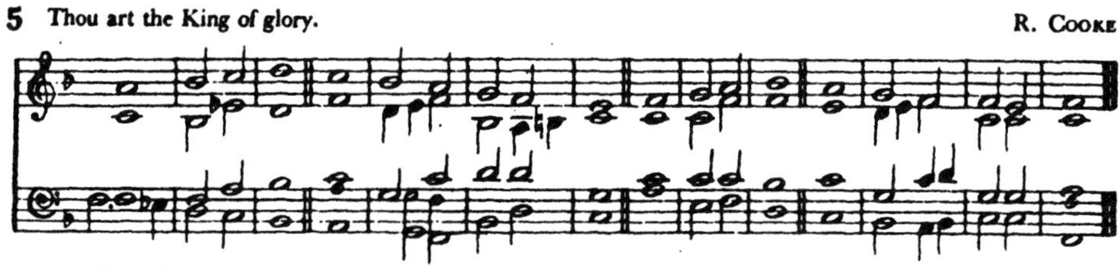

Original Key: G

6 O Lord, save thy people. J. Stainer

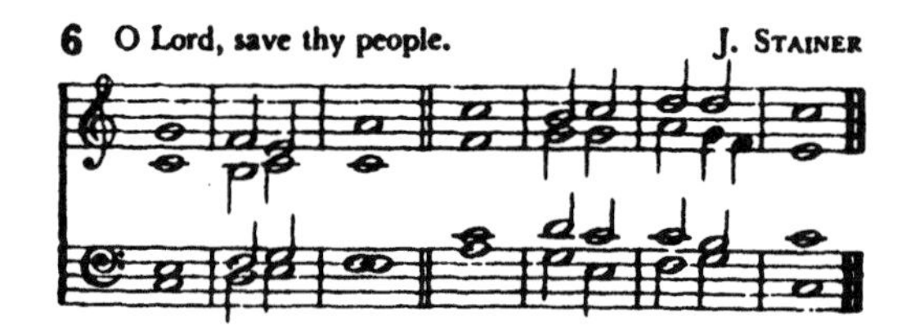

TE DEUM LAUDAMUS

THIRD SET

7 (also for Psalms 22, 47 and 54) J. DAVY

8 Thou art the King of glory. G. J. ELVEY

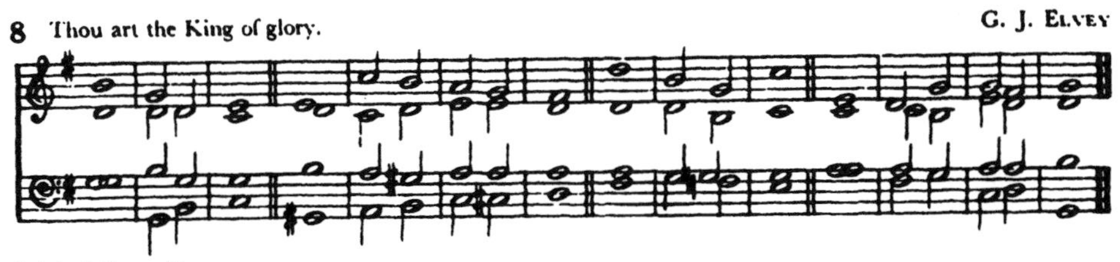

Original Key: A♭

9 O Lord, save thy people. H. BAKER

FOURTH SET

10 (also for Psalms 45, 104 and 132) J. L. HOPKINS

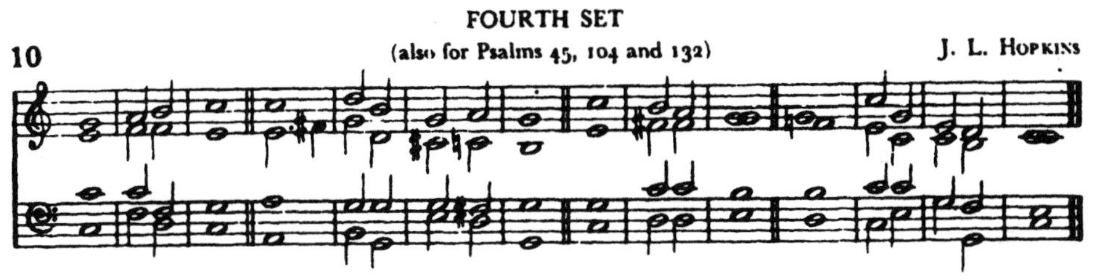

Original Key: D

11 Thou art the King of glory. R. COOKE

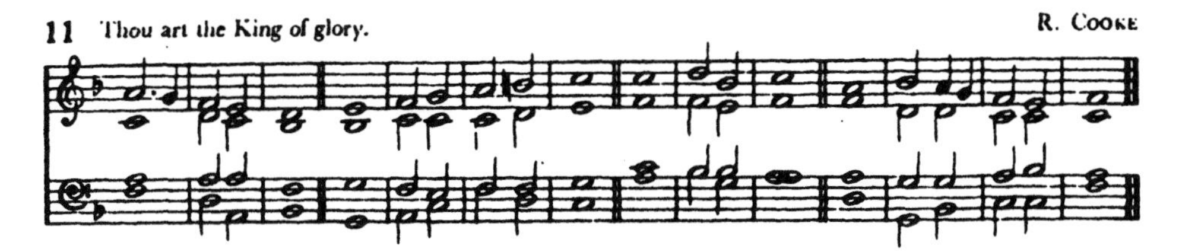

Original Key: G

12 O Lord, save thy people J. L. HOPKINS

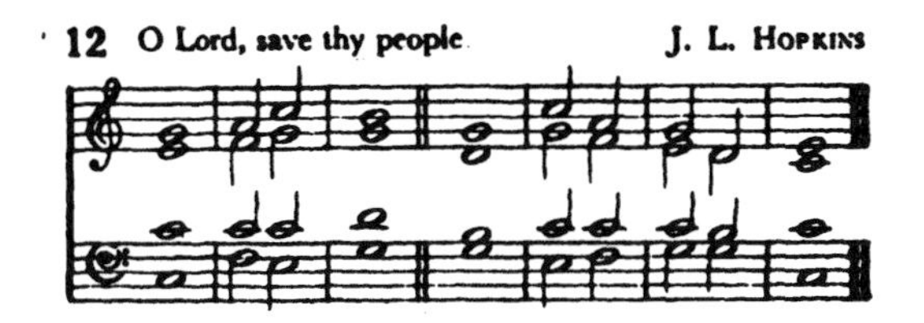

TE DEUM LAUDAMUS

FIFTH SET

13 (also for Psalms 18, 26 and 106) H. LAWES

Original Key: C

14 Thou art the King of glory. JOHN ROBINSON

15 O Lord, save thy people. D. B. EPERSON

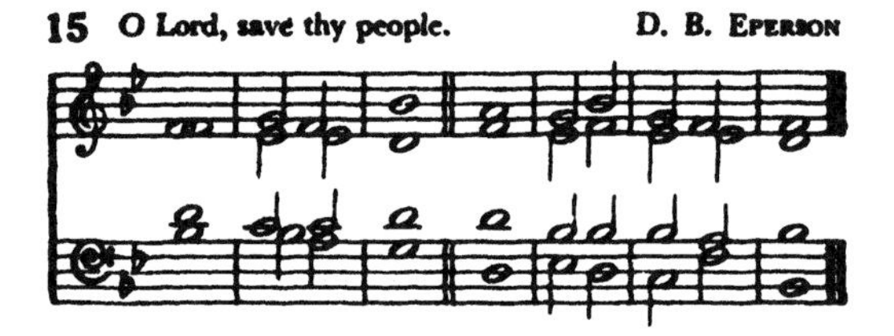

SIXTH SET

16 (QUADRUPLE CHANT)

H. S. OAKELEY

17 O Lord, save thy people. H. KEETON

(also for Psalm 127)

BENEDICITE, OMNIA OPERA

FIRST SET

verses 1 to 17 and 27 to end

18 W. RUSSELL

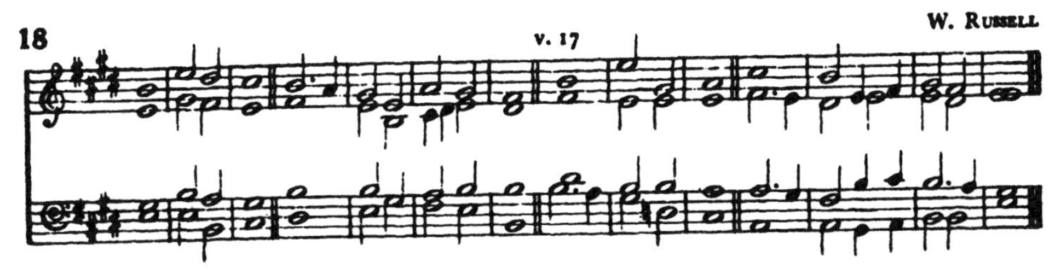

verses 18 to 26

19 T. A. WALMISLEY

(also for Psalm 105)

SECOND SET

verses 1 to 17 and 27 to end

20 M. CAMIDGE

(also for Psalm 44)

verses 18 to 26

21 F. A. G. OUSELEY

Also suitable: Chant 359

VENITE

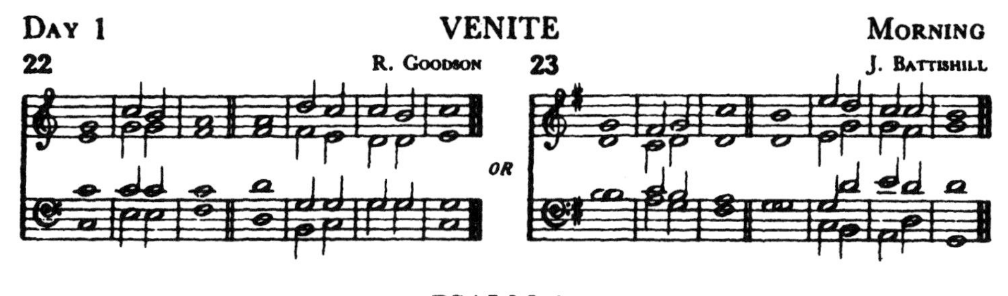

PSALM 1

PSALM 2

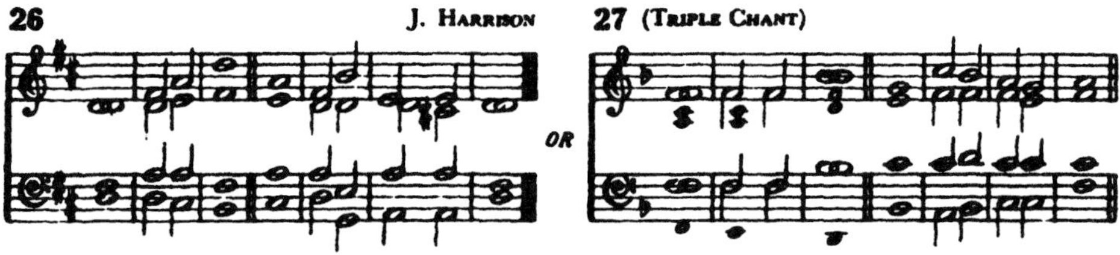

(When this chant is used in the daily course, Psalm 3 should be sung to Chant 29, and Psalm 4 to Chant 28).

PSALM 3

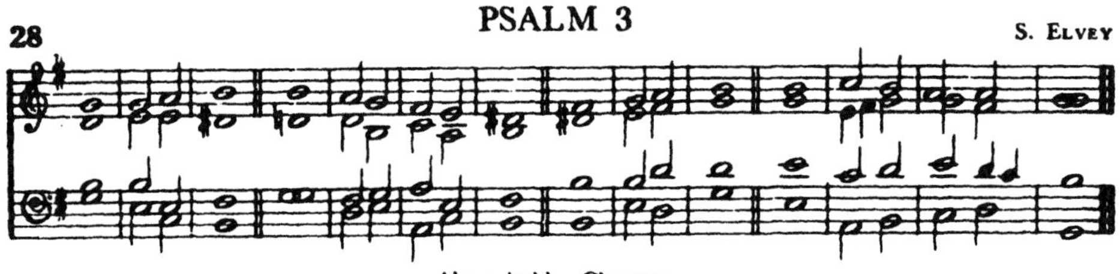

Also suitable : Chant 29

PSALM 4

Also suitable : Chant 28

PSALM 5

Original Key: F

Day 1

PSALM 6

Evening

PSALM 7

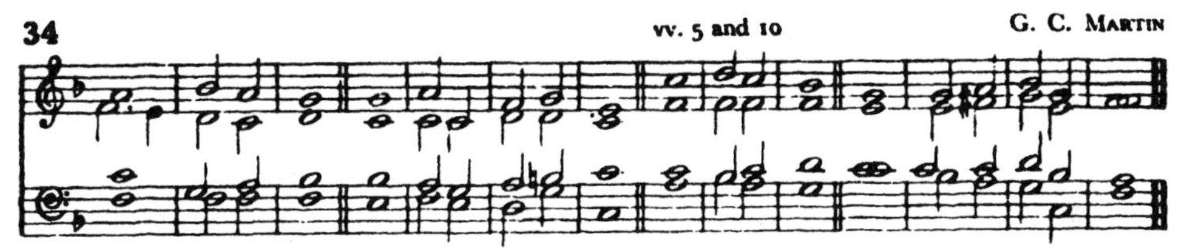

PSALM 8

Verses 1 and 9 may be sung in Unison.

OR

Verses 1 and 9 may be sung in Unison.

VENITE

37 E. G. MONK

Original Key: D

PSALM 9

38 W. KNYVETT (from HANDEL)

OR

39 J. GOSS

Original Key: F

PSALM 10

40 J. GOSS (from J. CLARKE)

Original Key: F♯ minor

PSALM 11

41 B. LUARD-SELBY

Original Key: B♭

42 H. Smart

PSALM 13

verses 1 to 4

43 P. Hayes

verse 5 to end

44 P. Hayes 45 F. A. G. Ouseley

PSALM 14

46* L. Flintoft

Original Key: G minor

* This and Chant 136 are the earliest examples of a double chant that have survived in general use: date, c. 1715.

47 G. A. MACFARREN

OR

48 T. TURTON

Original Key: G

PSALM 15

49 T. KELWAY

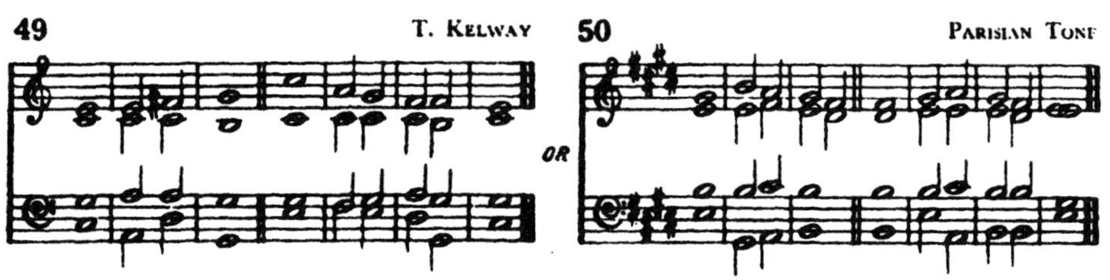

Original Key: D

OR

50 PARISIAN TONE

PSALM 16

51 W. CROTCH

OR

52 J. FOSTER

PSALM 17

53 (S) vv. 5 and 12 J. TURLE

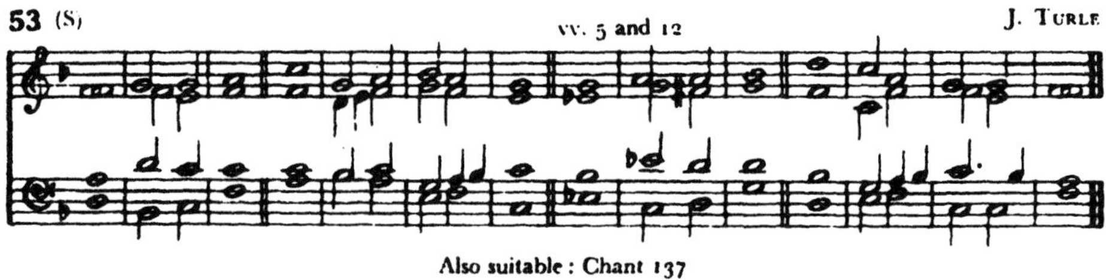

Also suitable: Chant 137

verses 1 to 30 and 47 to end

54 (S) vv. 15, 24 and 31 J. TURLE

Original Key: A

Alternative chant for verses 7 to 15:

55 v. 15 J. GOSS

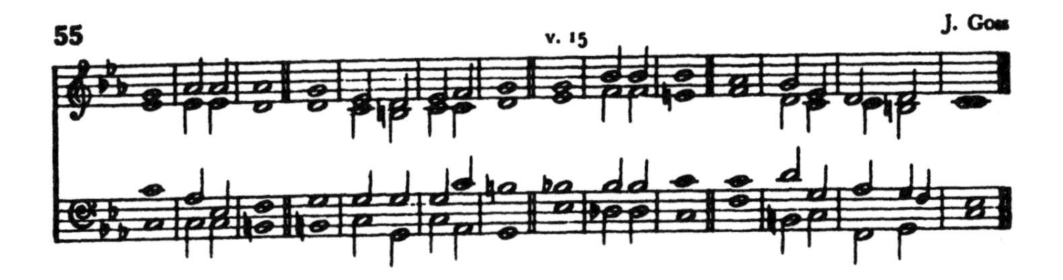

56 verses 31 to 46 JOHN ROBINSON

57 J. ALCOCK **58** F. A. G. OUSELEY

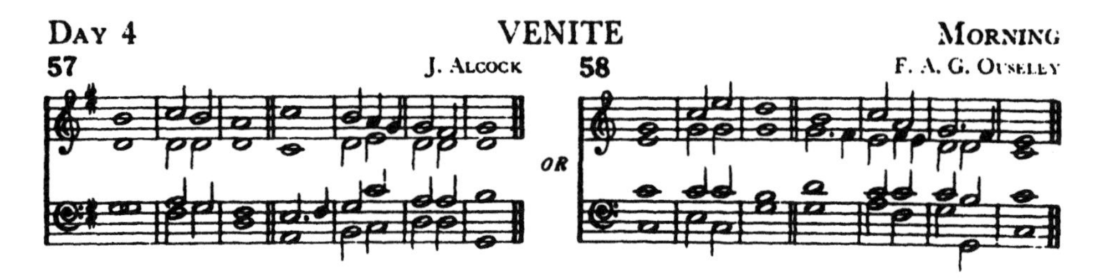

PSALM 19

verses 1 to 6 and Gloria

59 E. G. MONK

Original Key: D

OR

60 verses 1 to 6 and Gloria W. BOYCE

verses 7 to 15

61 E. HODGSON

PSALM 20

62 H. ALDRICH **63** L. L. DIX

Original Key: A

PSALM 21

64 J. GOSS

PSALM 22

verses 1 to 21

65 M. CAMIDGE

verse 22 to end

66* M. CAMIDGE

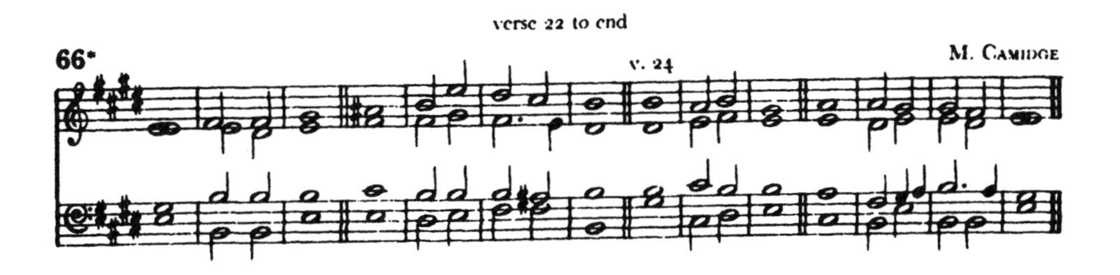

OR

verse 22 to end

67 G. J. ELVEY

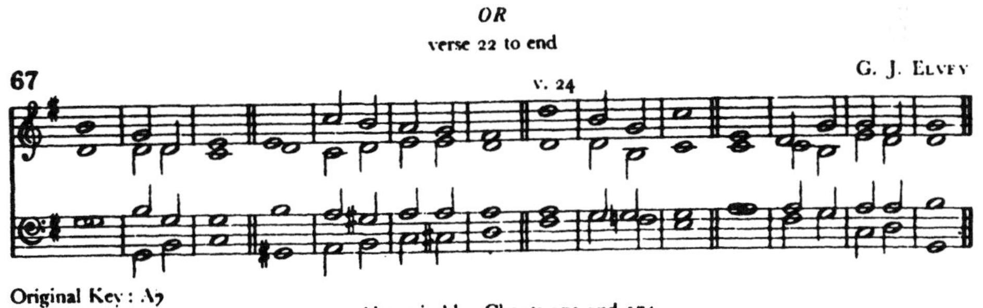

Original Key: A♭

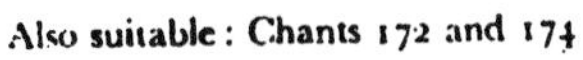

Also suitable: Chants 172 and 174

PSALM 23

68 (S) J. TURLE

OR

69 (S) C. H. LLOYD

OR

70 (S) E. S. CARTER

Also suitable: Chants 132 and 362

*Adapted from the minor chant by S. Elvey.

VENITE

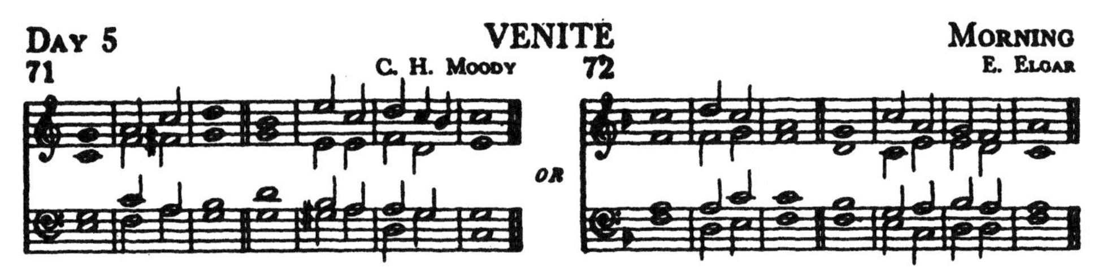

Original Key: G

PSALM 24

Verses 7 to 10 may be sung in Unison, the first half of verses 8 and 10 being sung by Trebles only or by Tenors and Basses only.

OR

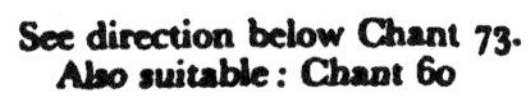
See direction below Chant 73.
Also suitable: Chant 60

PSALM 25

PSALM 26

OR

78 verses 1 to 7 and Gloria — J. STAINER

79 (S) verses 8 to 16 — C. HYLTON STEWART

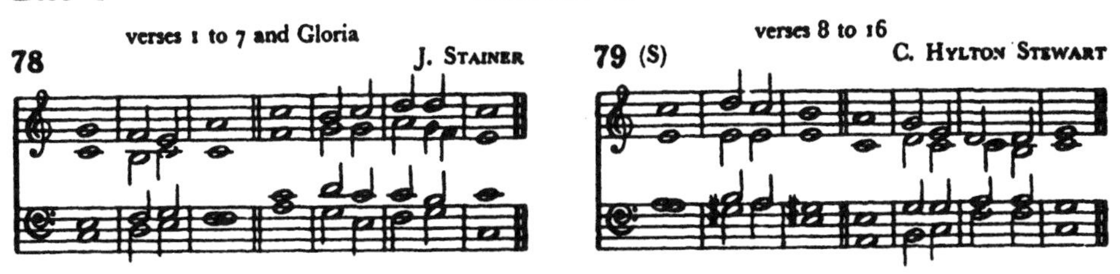

Original Key: D

OR

80 verses 1 to 7 and Gloria — W. H. LONGHURST

Original Key: C

81 verses 8 to 16 — J. BARNBY

PSALM 28

82 (S) verses 1 to 6 — C. HYLTON STEWART

83 verse 7 to end — E. J. HOPKINS

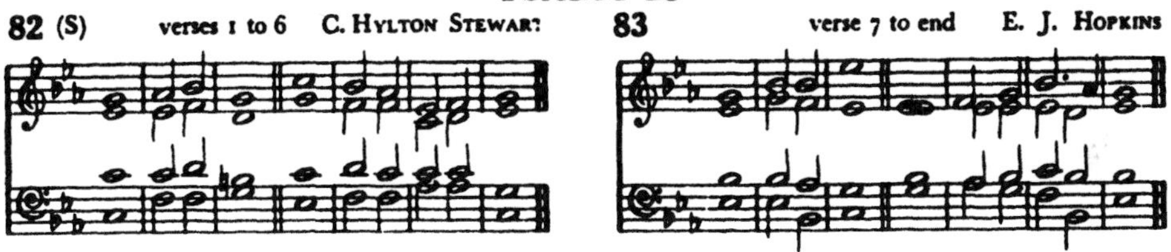

PSALM 29

84 T. ATTWOOD

OR

85 G. A. MACFARREN

Original Key: C

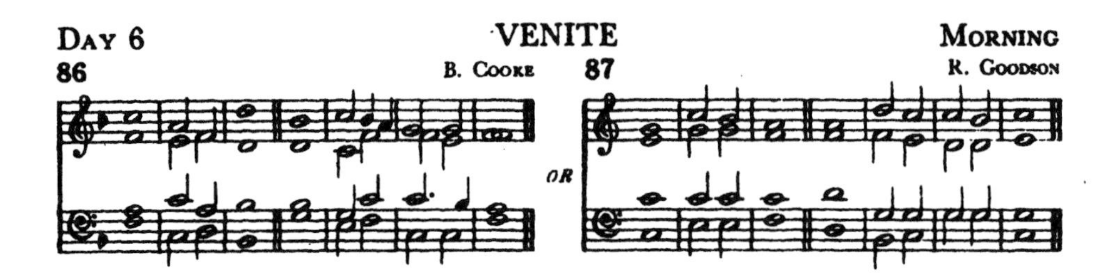

PSALM 30

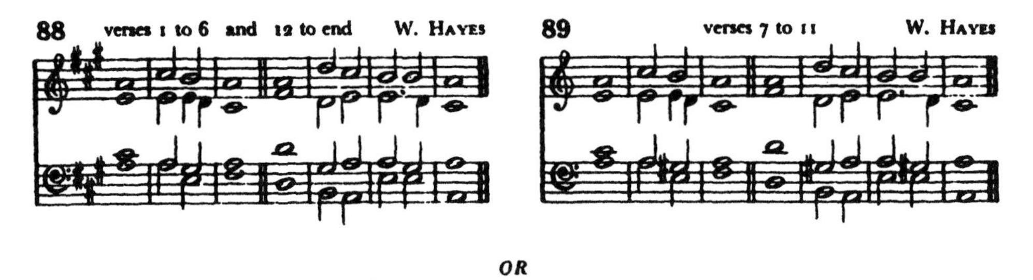

OR

verses 1 to 6 and 12 to end

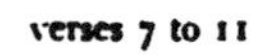

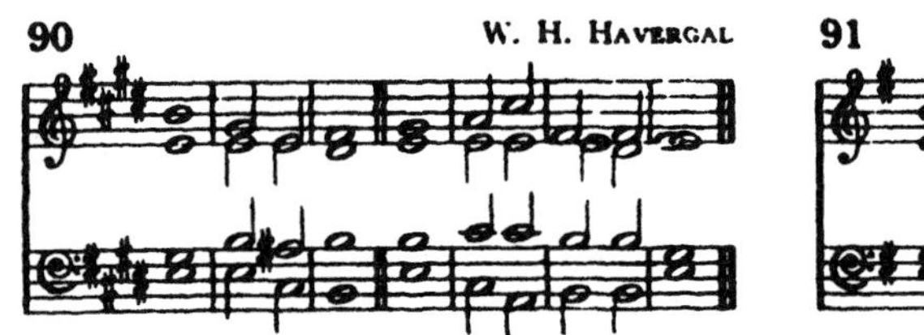

PSALM 31

verses 1 to 9 and 21 to end

verses 10 to 20

Original Key: A minor

94

S. ELVEY

OR

95

J. M. FOX

PSALM 33

96

J. TURLE

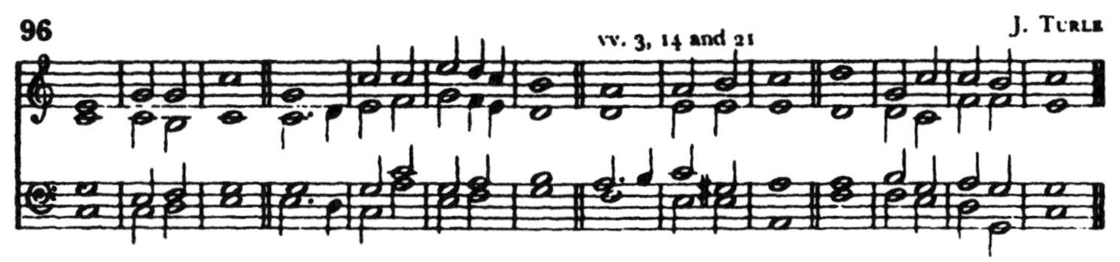

Also suitable · Chant 123

PSALM 34

97

F. A. G. OUSELEY

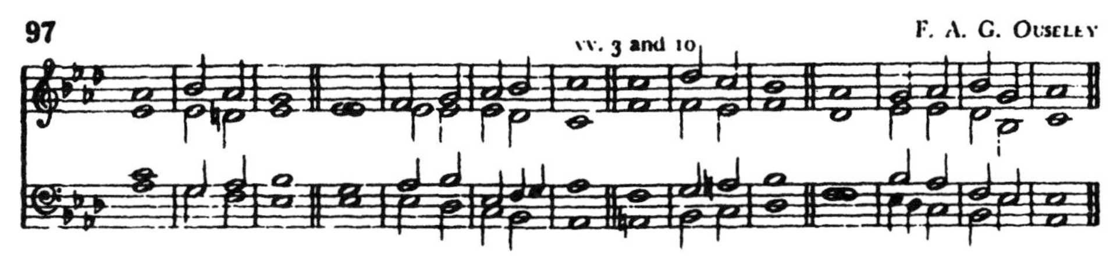

OR

98

J. BARNBY

vv. 3 and 10

Original Key: E

99 J. Goss

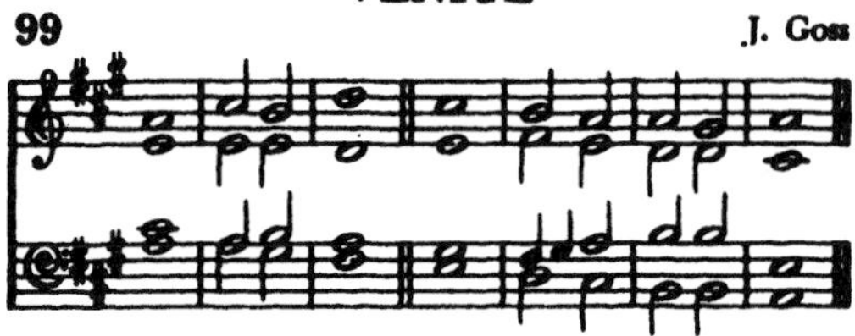

PSALM 35

verses 1 to 8 and 11 to 26

100 A. H. Man

verses 9 and 10 and 27 to end

101 C. F. South

OR

(for the whole Psalm)

102 (S) P. Armes

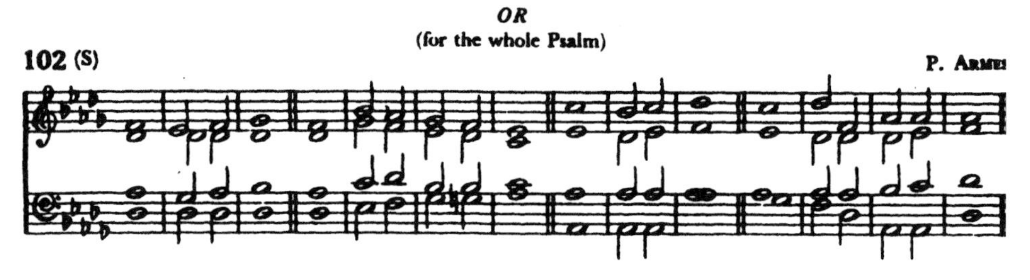

PSALM 36

103 verses 1 to 4 W. Croft

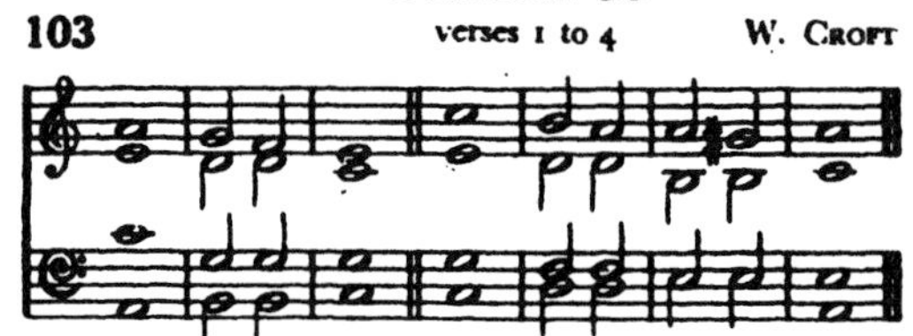

verse 5 to end

104 Stephens *OR* 105 H. G. Ley

Original Key: B♭

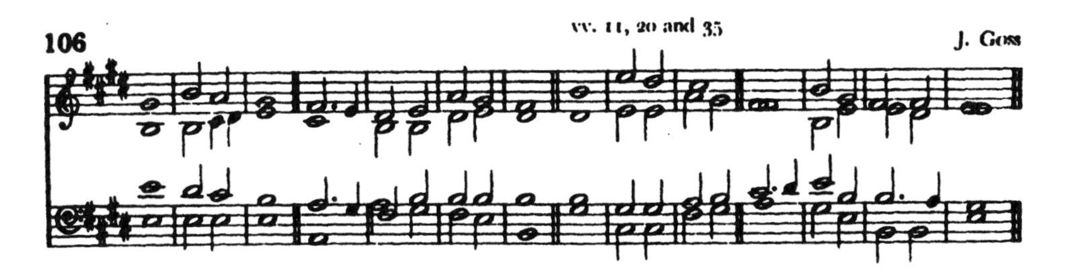

OR

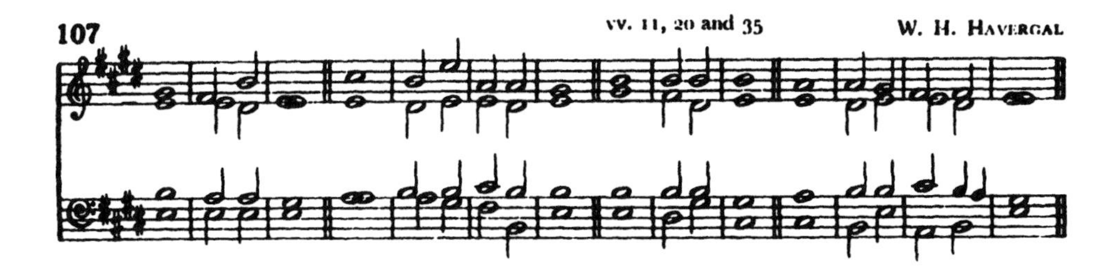

Original Key: D

PSALM 38

Original Key: D minor

(On Ash Wednesday morning, after Psalm 32, this chant should be played in C♯ minor).

Also suitable: Chant 345

PSALM 39

Also suitable: Chant 150

PSALM 40

OR

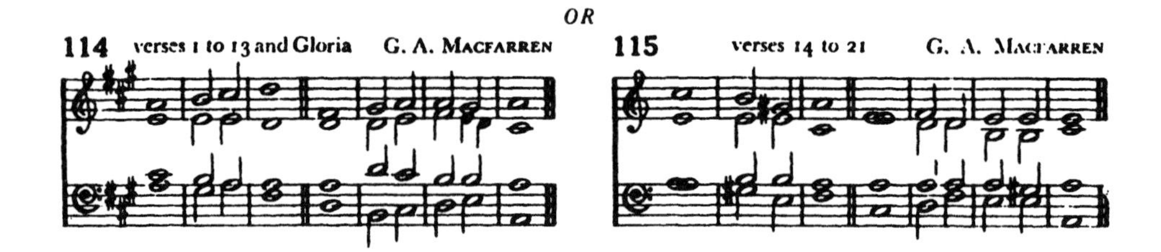

PSALM 41

116 F. A. G. OUSELEY

Verse 13 may be sung in Unison.

OR

117 (TRIPLE CHANT) J. NAYLOR

Verse 13 may be sung in Unison.

Alternative chant for the Doxology (verse 13), which may be used with either of the above chants:

118 E. F. RIMBAULT

PSALMS 42 and 43

(which should be sung as one Psalm, the Gloria being omitted after Psalm 42).

119 v. 5 (Ps. 42) S. WESLEY

Verses 6 and 7, 14 and 15, and verses 5 and 6 of Psalm 43 may be sung in Unison, the first verse of each pair being sung by Trebles only or by Tenors and Basses only.

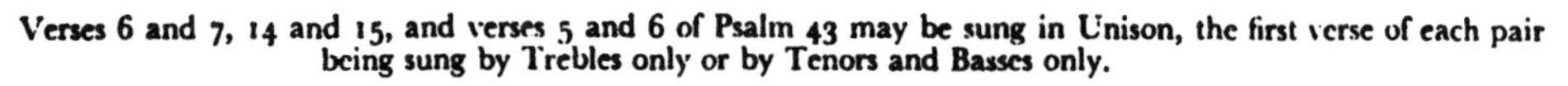

OR

120 v. 5 (Ps. 42) J. TURLE

See direction below Chant 119.

121 S. ELVEY OR 122 CORFE

PSALM 44

verses 1 to 9 and Gloria

123 M. CAMIDGE

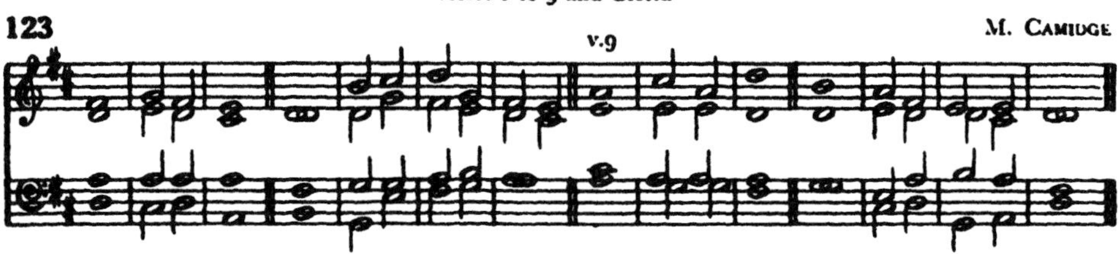

Original Key: E♭

verses 10 to 26

124 J. BARNBY

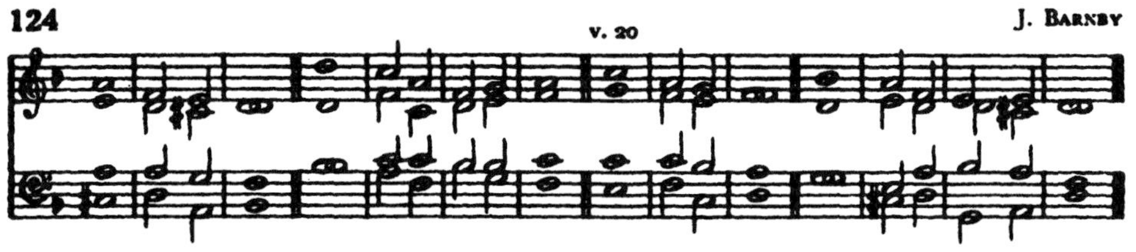

Also suitable: Chants 172 and 174

PSALM 45

125 verses 1 to 10 and 17 to end R. COOKE

Original Key: G

126 verses 11 to 16 G. A. MACFARREN

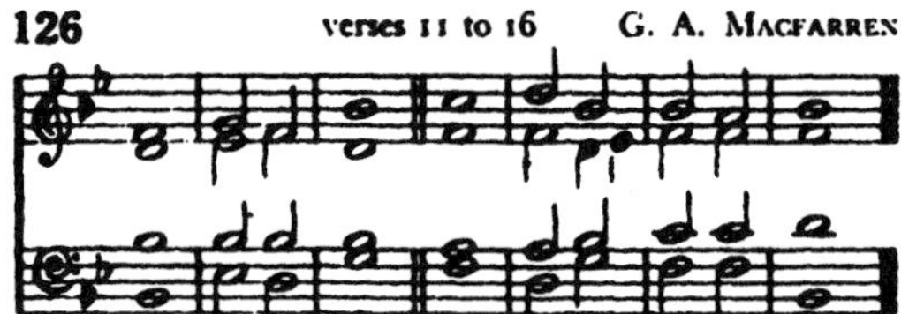

PSALM 46

127 From M. LUTHER

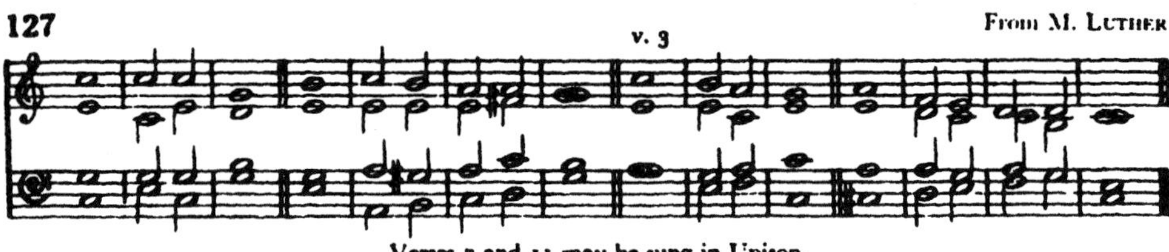

Verses 7 and 11 may be sung in Unison.

128 (S) J. TURLE

OR

129 J. DAVY

PSALM 48

130 H. SMART

OR

131 W. J. MOTHERSOLE

Original Key: A

PSALM 49

132 (S) T. A. WALMISLEY

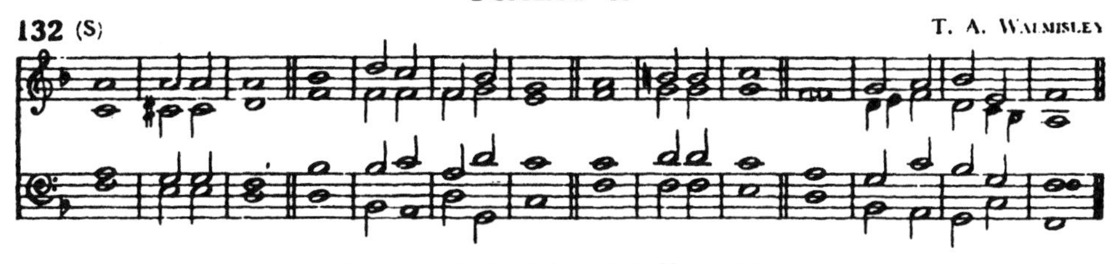

Verses 12 and 20 may be sung in Unison (*p*).

PSALM 50

Also suitable: Chant 317

PSALM 51

Also suitable: Chants 139, 147, 162 and 197

PSALM 52

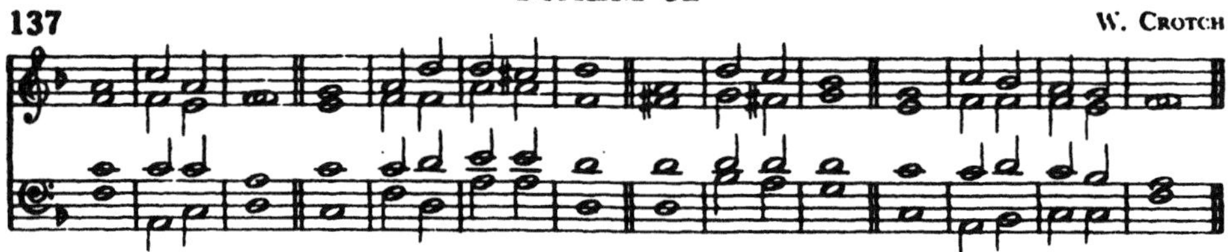

OR

* This and Chant 139 are the earliest examples of a double chant that have survived in general use: date, c. 1715.

PSALM 53

139*

L. FLINTOFT

Original Key: G minor

PSALM 54

140

E. F. RIMBAULT

OR

141

H. BAKER

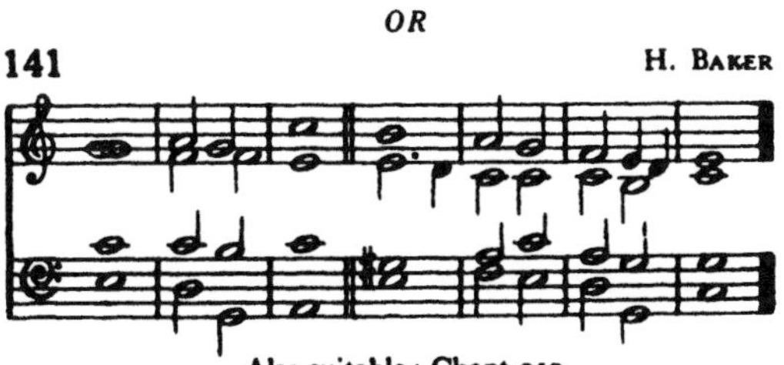

Also suitable: Chant 210

PSALM 55

142

vv. 11, 16 and 25

J. GOSS

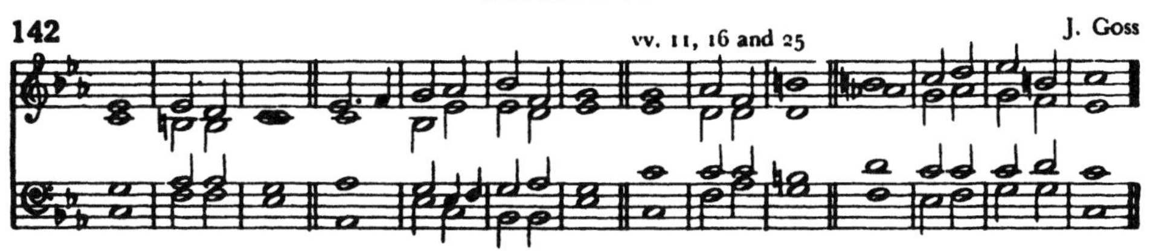

OR

143

vv. 11, 16 and 25

J. GOSS (from J. CLARKE)

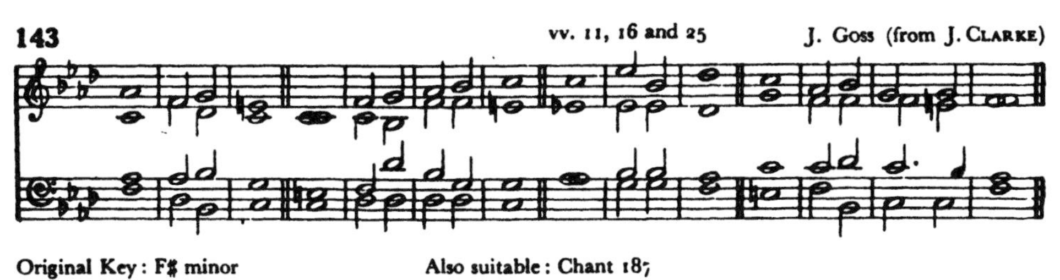

Original Key: F♯ minor

Also suitable: Chant 187

*See footnote on opposite page.

VENITE

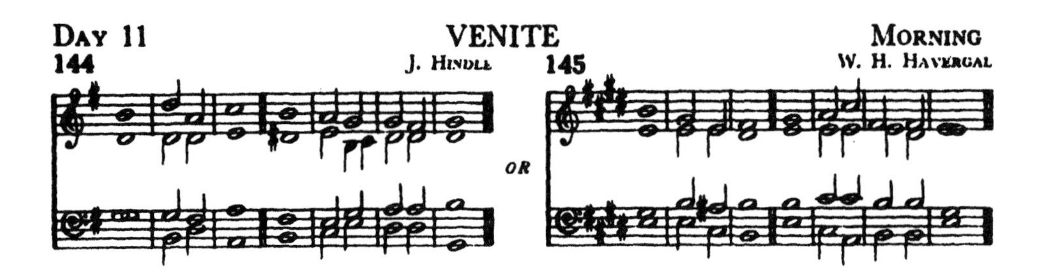

PSALM 56

Also suitable: Chant 368

PSALM 57

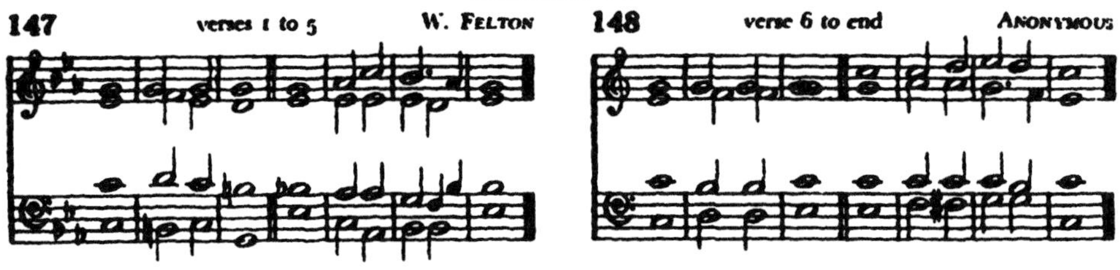

Verses 6 and 12 may be sung in Unison.

PSALM 58

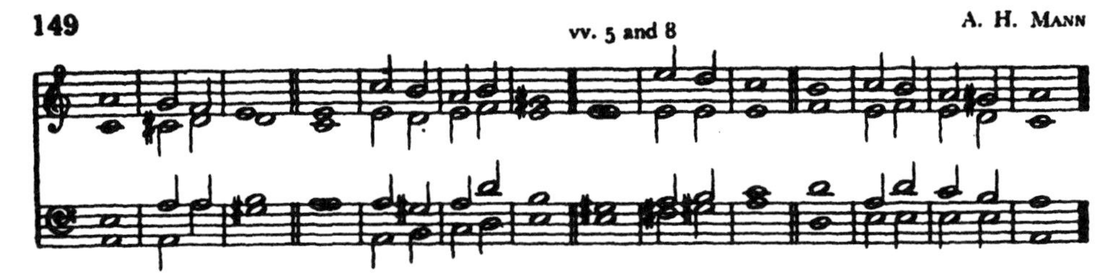

150 J. BARNBY

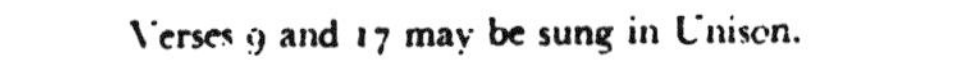
Verses 9 and 17 may be sung in Unison.

Alternative chant for verse 16 to end (and also, if desired, for verses 8 and 9):

151 C. F. SOUTH

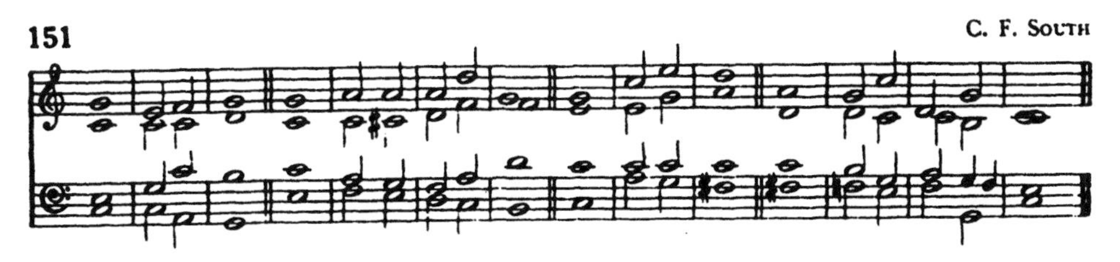

PSALM 60

152 verses 1 to 4 S. S. WESLEY

153 verse 5 to end F. A. G. OUSELEY

PSALM 61

154 H. G. LEY

OR

155 T. TOMKINS

VENITE

156 D. B. EPERSON

OR

157 W. RUSSELL

PSALM 62

158 J. JONES

Verses 1 and 2, and 5 and 6 may be sung in Unison.

159 (S) *OR* W. PARRATT

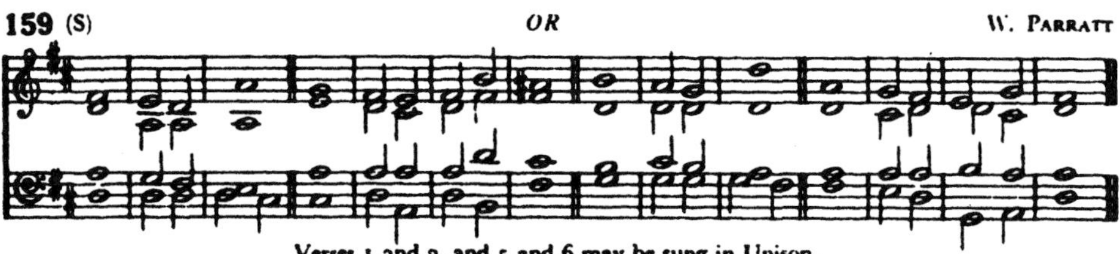

Verses 1 and 2, and 5 and 6 may be sung in Unison.

PSALM 63

160 J. CAMIDGE (Junr.)

OR

161 (S) W. MONK

Also suitable: Chant 28

PSALM 64

162 G. M. GARRETT

PSALM 65

163 T. A. Walmisley

OR

164 G. M. Garrett

Also suitable: Chant 96

PSALM 66

165 vv. 11 and 16 G. J. Elvey

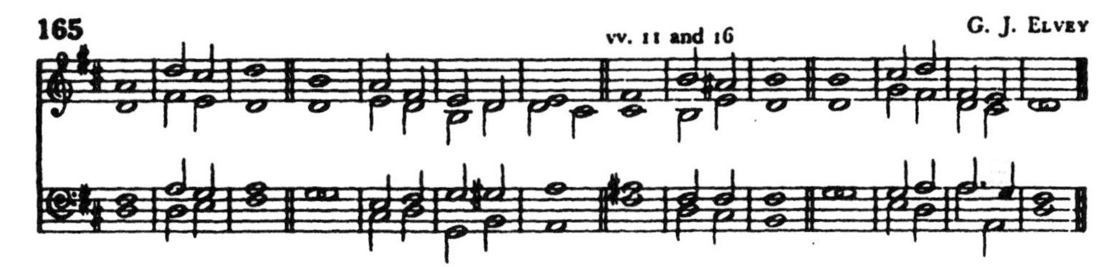

PSALM 67

166 J. Nares *OR* **167** G. A. Slater

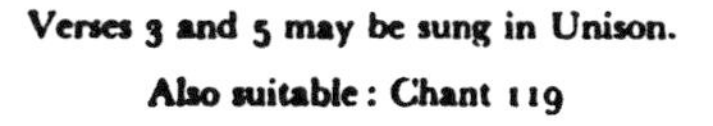

Verses 3 and 5 may be sung in Unison.

Also suitable: Chant 119

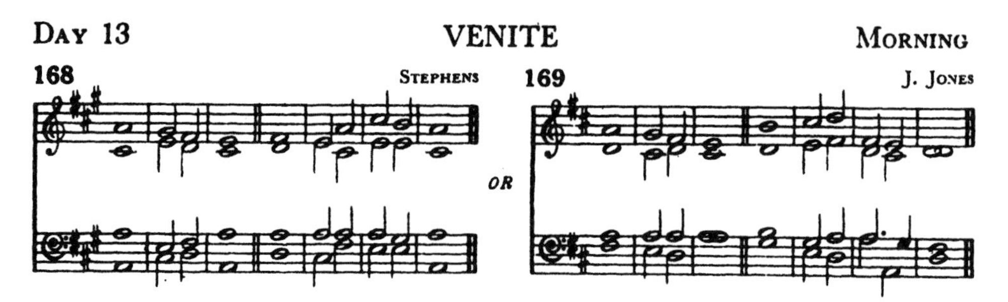

Original Key: B♭

PSALM 68

OR

171 v. 23 J. GOSS

Original Key: A

Also suitable: Chants 125 and 264

verses 1 to 29

172 J. Battishill

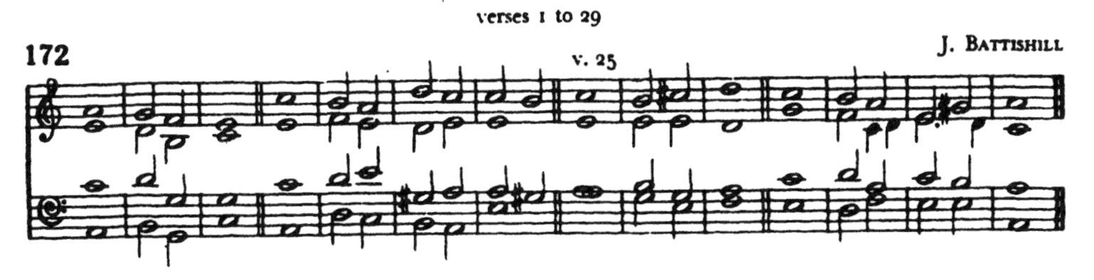

Alternative chant for verses 23 to 29:

173 Walford Davies

verse 30 to end

174 J. Battishill

OR

verse 30 to end

175 E. T. Chipp

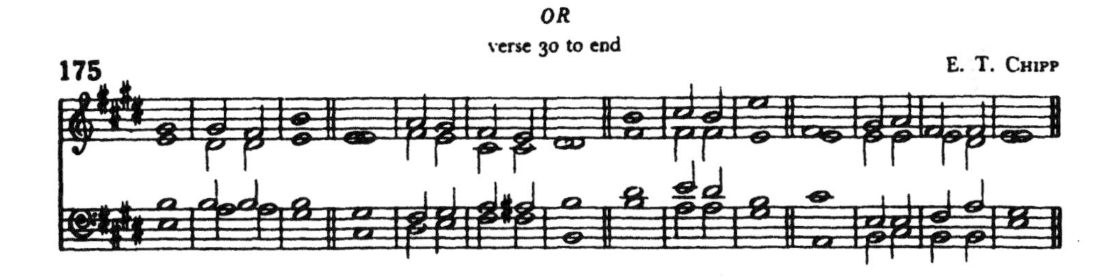

PSALM 70

176 G. A. Macfarren

OR

177 (S) C. C. Palmer

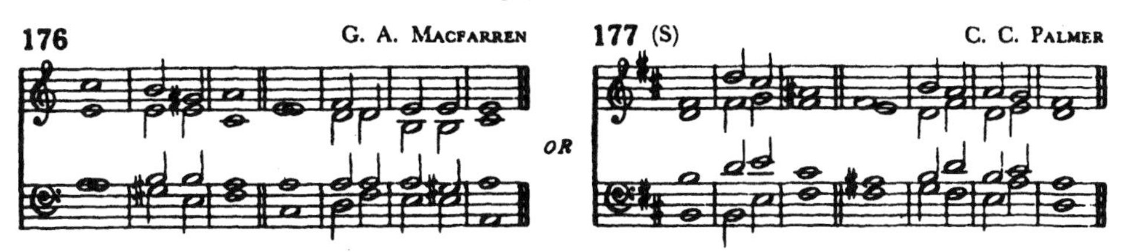

178 E. G. Monk — **179** D. B. Everson

PSALM 71

180 vv. 5 and 14 — I. A. Atkins

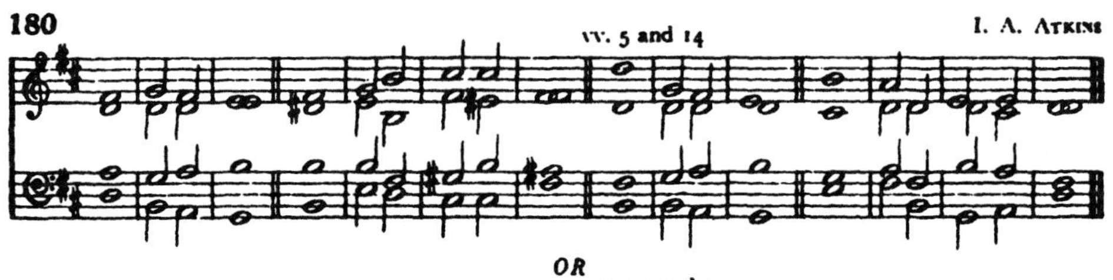

OR

181 vv. 5 and 14 — G. Cooper

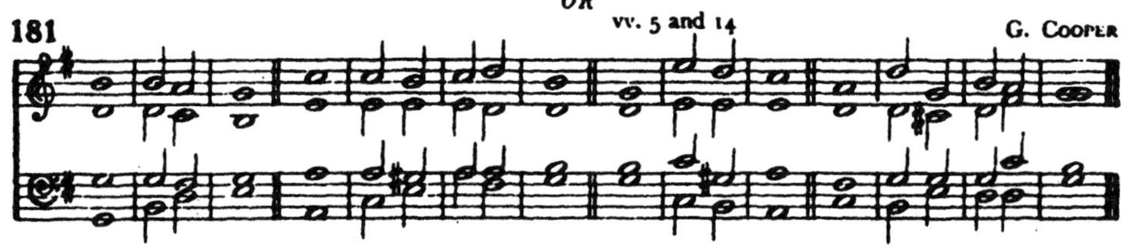

PSALM 72

182 vv. 5, 14 and 17 — H. G. Ley

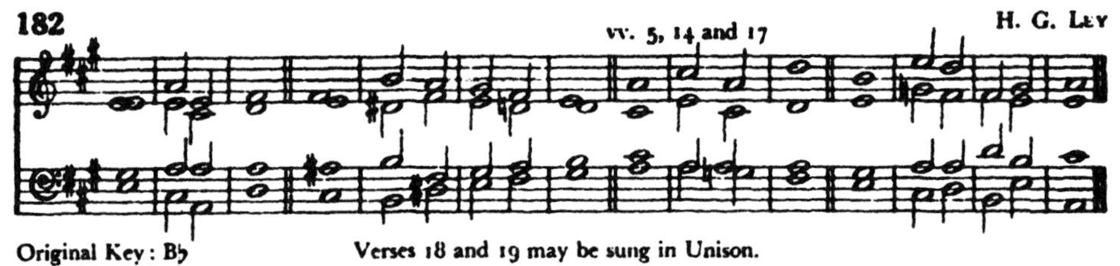

Original Key: B♭ — Verses 18 and 19 may be sung in Unison.

OR

183 vv. 5, 14 and 17 — E. Cutler

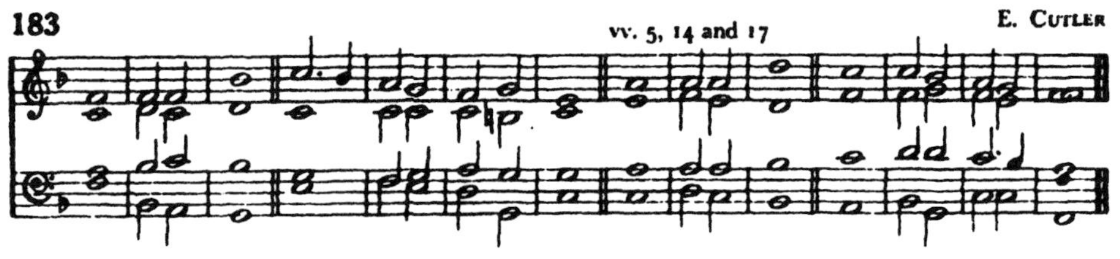

Original Key: G — Verses 18 and 19 may be sung in Unison.

Also suitable: Chant 35

Alternative chant for the Doxology (verses 18 and 19), which may be used with either of the above chants:

184 E. F. Rimbault

185 J. BARNBY

Alternative chant for verse 22 to end:

186 J. SOAPER

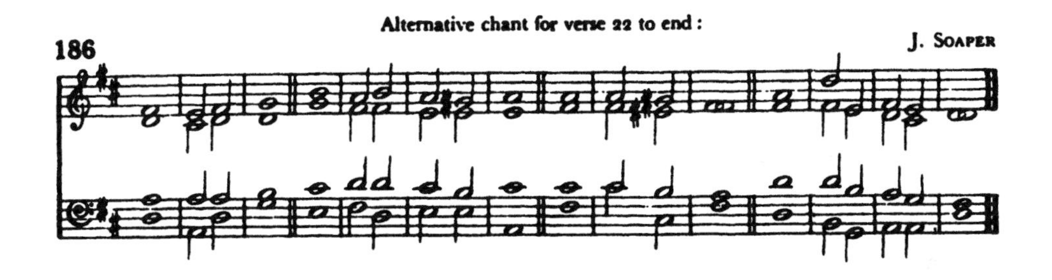

PSALM 74

187 J. TURLE

Alternative chant for verses 13 to 18 and Gloria:

188 J. TURLE

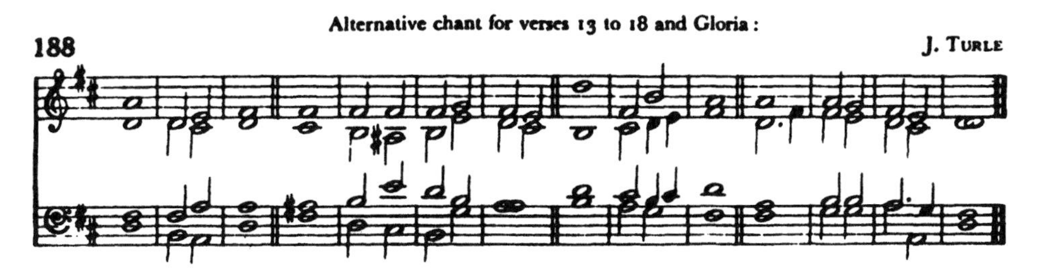

Also suitable: Chants 65 and 66

189 G. A. MACFARREN **190** J. BATTISHILL

PSALM 75

191 T. A. WALMISLEY

PSALM 76

192 V. NOVELLO **193** (TRIPLE CHANT) J. NAYLOR

Also suitable: Chant 336

PSALM 77

verses 1 to 9

194 S. S. WESLEY

verse 10 to end

195 C. E. MILLER

verses 1 to 10, 13 to 17, 38 to 40 and 53 to 56

196* M. CAMIDGE

vv. 17 and 40

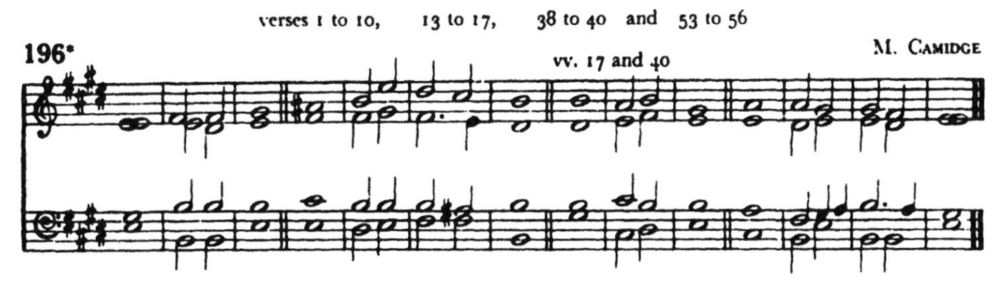

verses 11 and 12, 18 to 21, 32 to 37, 41 to 52 and 57 to 59

197 M. CAMIDGE

v. 59

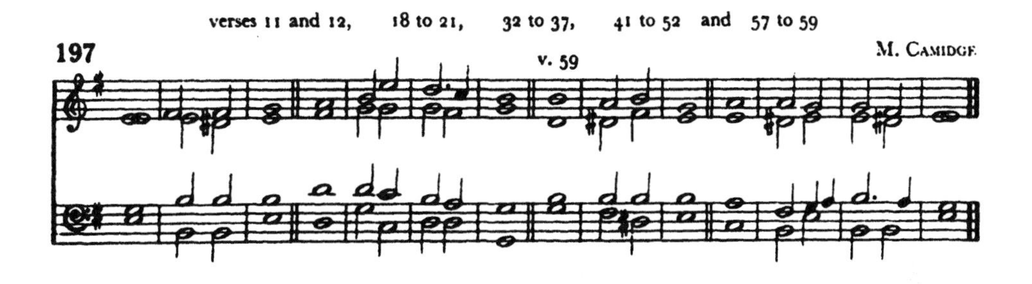

verses 22 to 31 and 60 to 65

198 L. L. DIX

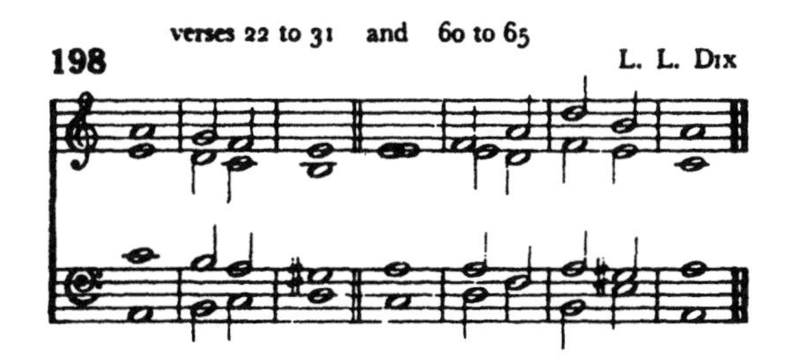

verse 66 to end

199 T. ATTWOOD

Original Key: D

Also suitable (for the whole Psalm): Chant 16

*Adapted from the minor chant by S. Elvey.

VENITE

200 G. M. GARRETT OR 201 E. G. MONK

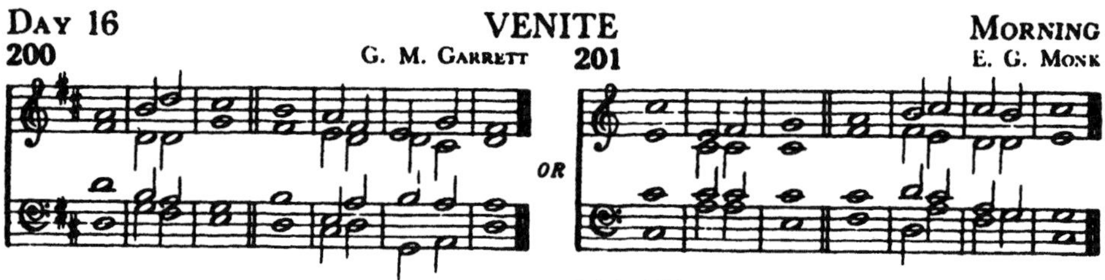

Original Key: D

PSALM 79

202 J. GOSS

OR

203 F. W. WADELY

PSALM 80

204 vv. 3, 16 and 19 T. ATTWOOD

Verses 3, 7 and 19 may be sung in Unison (*p*).

PSALM 81

verses 1 to 11 and Gloria

205 vv. 3, 8 and 11 H. G. LEY

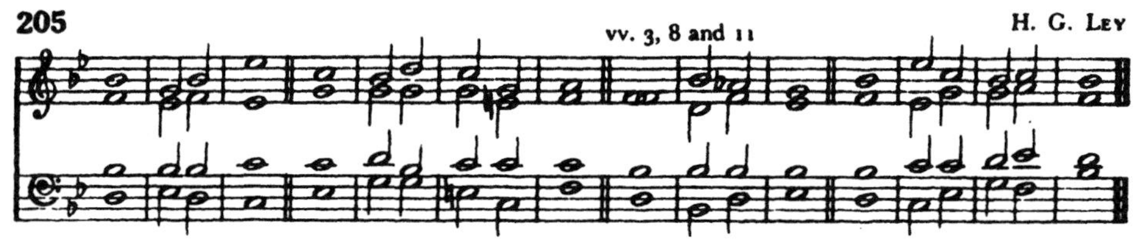

verses 12 to 17

206 T. KELWAY

PSALM 82

207 — C. Gibbons

OR

208 — S. S. Wesley

PSALM 83

209 — C. V. Stanford

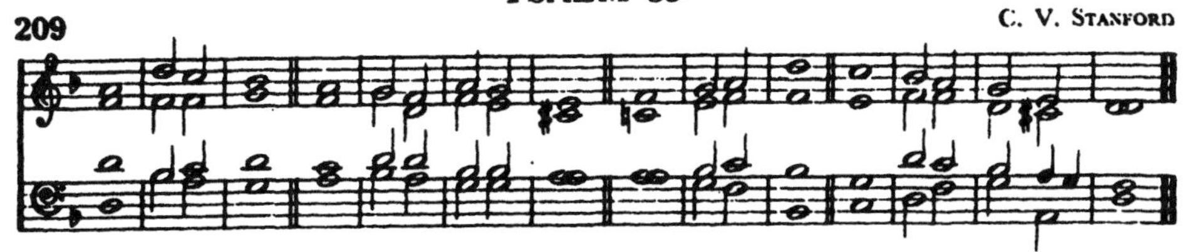

PSALM 84

210 — G. C. Martin

OR

211 — E. C. Bairstow

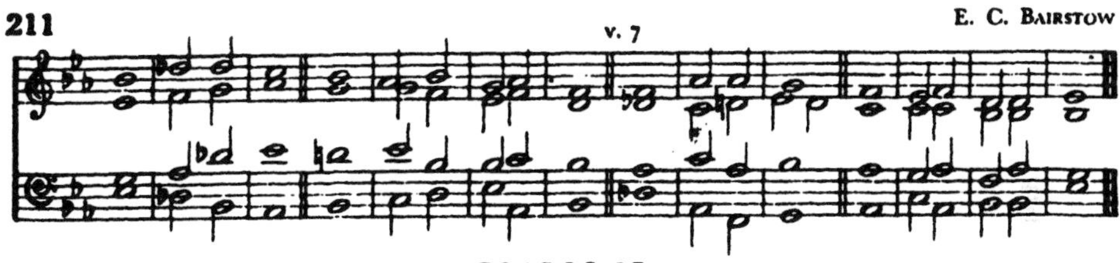

PSALM 85

212 — verses 1 to 3 and 8 to end — H. Smart

213 — verses 4 to 7 — J. Naylor

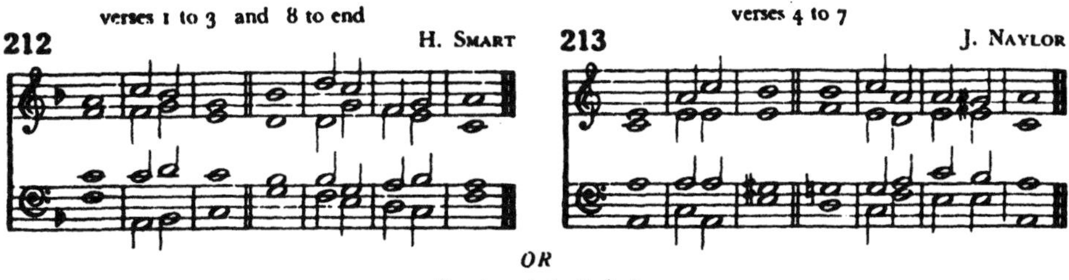

OR

(for the whole Psalm)

214 (S) — G. C. Martin

VENITE

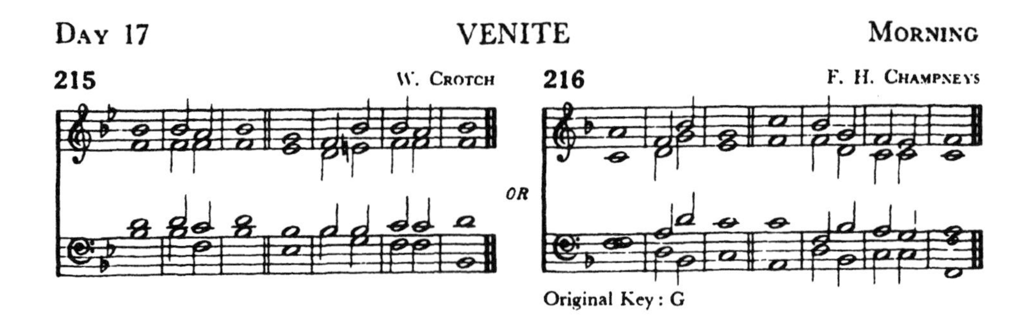

Original Key: G

PSALM 86

PSALM 87

PSALM 88

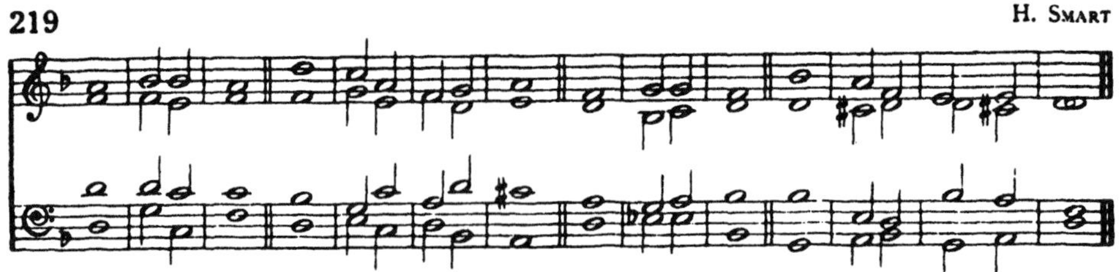

PSALM 89

verses 1 to 36 and Gloria

220 E. J. HOPKINS

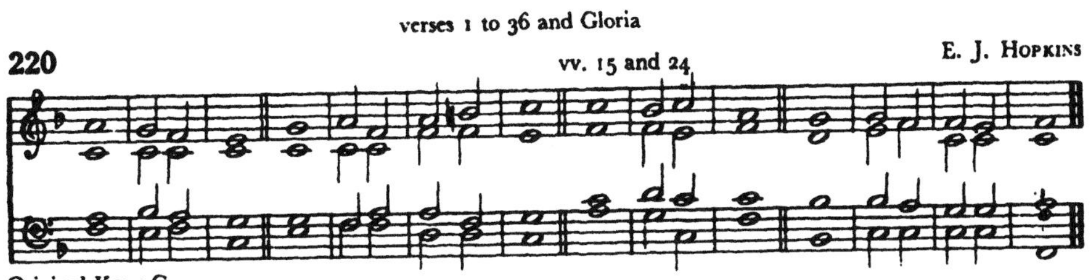

Original Key: G

Alternative chant for verses 5 to 19:

221 W. RUSSELL

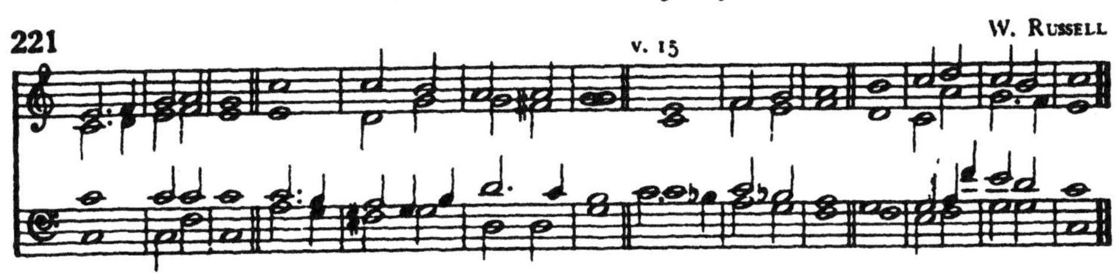

verses 37 to 50a

222 E. J. HOPKINS

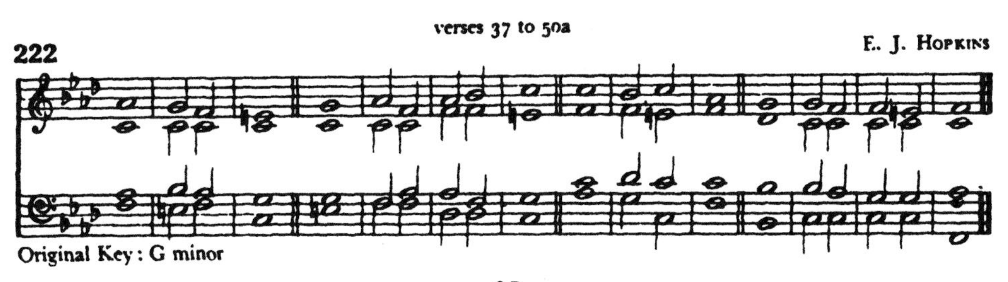

Original Key: G minor

OR

verses 37 to 50a

223 (S) W. PRENDERGAST

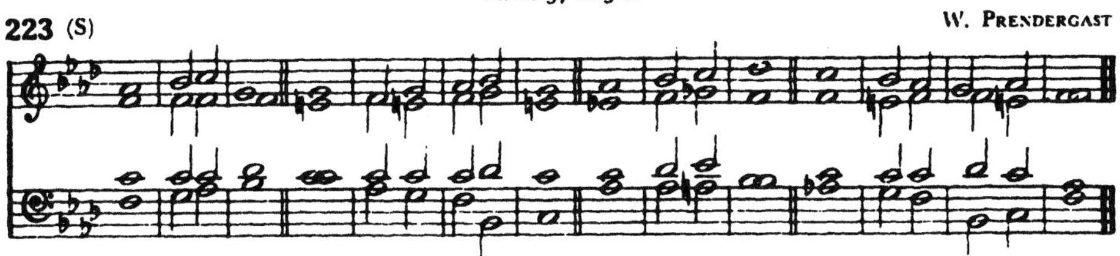

verse 50b (the Doxology)

224 E. J. HOPKINS

OR

225 E. F. RIMBAULT

This may be sung in Unison.

VENITE

226 W. Russell

227 Reginald A. Atkins

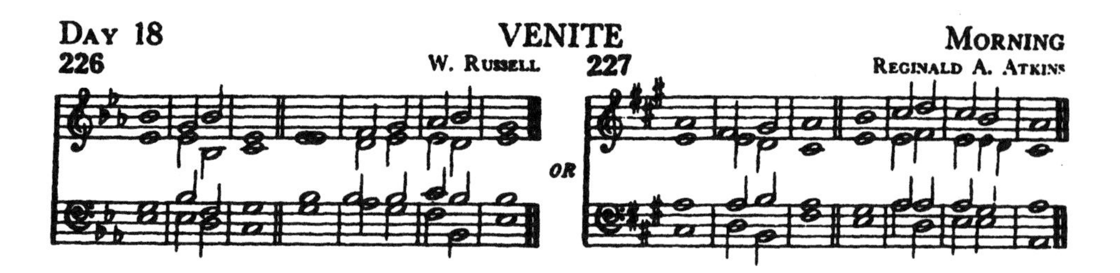

PSALM 90

228 J. Barnby

OR

229 (S) F. W. Wadely

PSALM 91

230 'Trent'

Also suitable: Chant 339

PSALM 92

231 G. J. Elvey

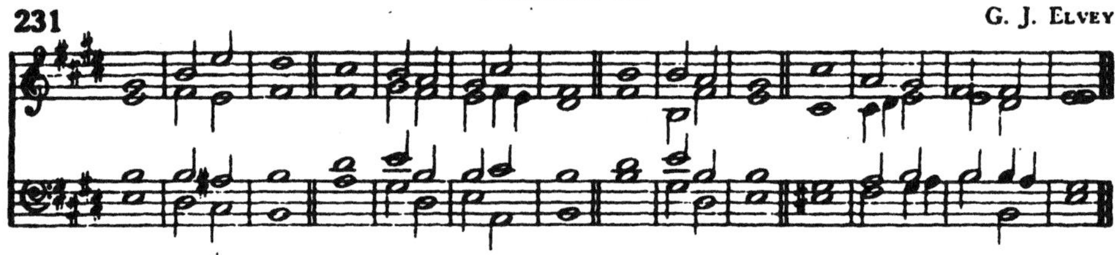

OR

232 P. C. Buck

PSALM 93

OR

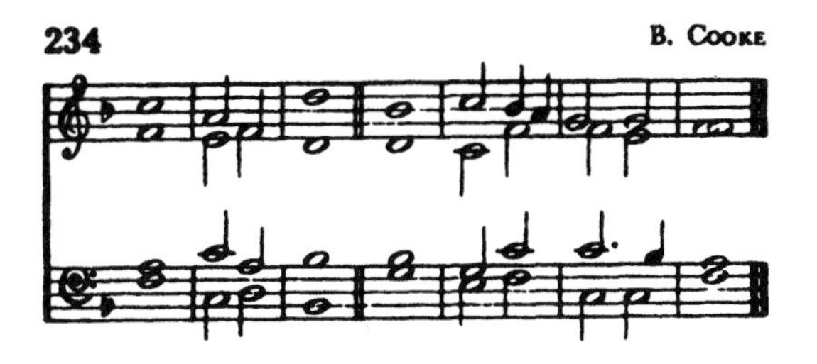

PSALM 94

verses 1 to 11

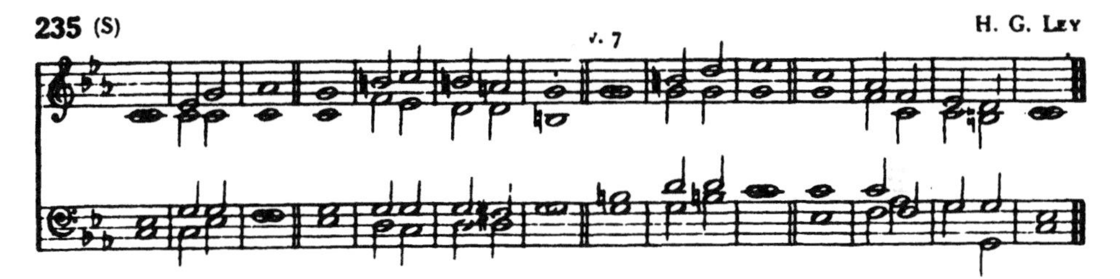

verse 12 to end

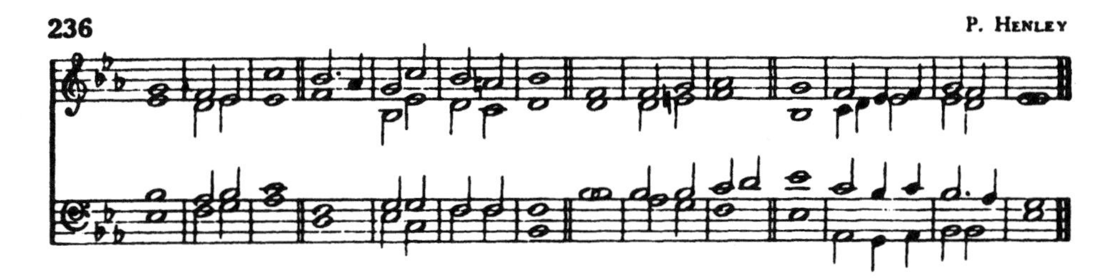

PSALM 95
(VENITE)

PSALM 96

239* E. G. MONK

Original Key: A♭

OR

240 (S) (TRIPLE CHANT)

H. M. HAVERGAL

PSALM 97

241 G. T. THALBEN-BALL OR 242 W. HAYES

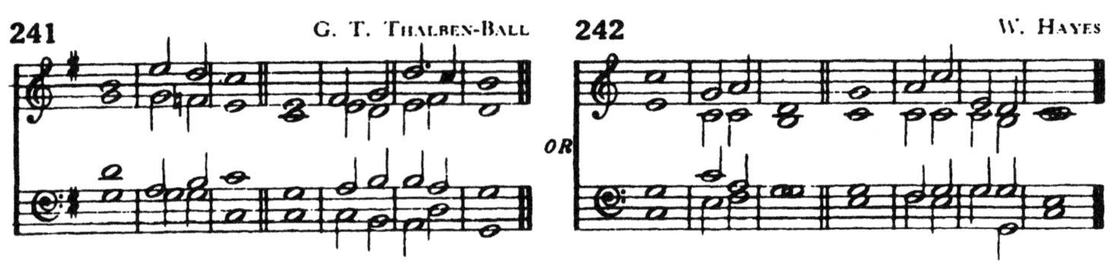

Original Key: D

*Although the verses of Psalm 96 are in groups of three, it is possible to sing the Psalm to a double chant without obscuring the sense.

PSALM 98

Original Key: A♭

PSALM 99

Original Key: B♭

Verses 5 and 9 may be sung in Unison.

PSALM 100

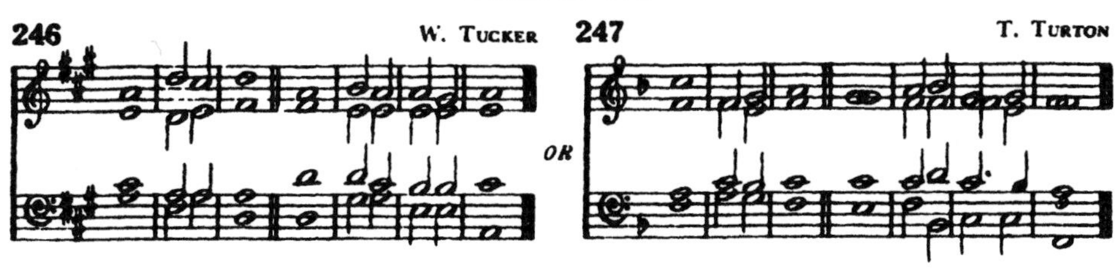

Original Key: G

PSALM 101

OR

250 B. LUARD-SELBY

OR

251 A. BROWN

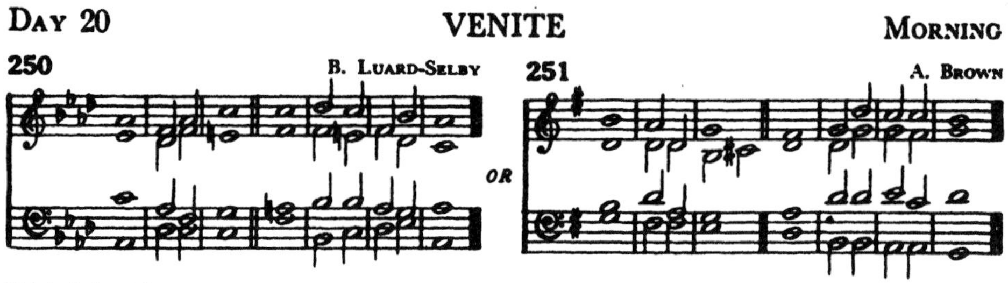

Original Key: B♭

Original Key: A♭

PSALM 102

verses 1 to 11

252 H. STONEX

v. 7

Original Key: F♯ minor

verse 12 to end

253 J. GOSS

v. 14

Original Key: B♭

PSALM 103

254 S. WESLEY

vv. 5 and 10

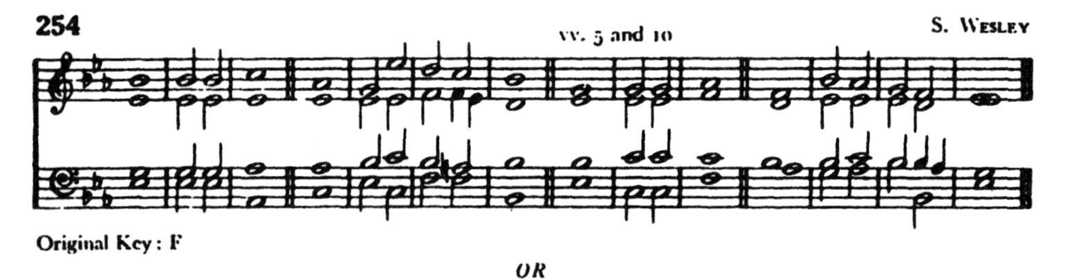

Original Key: F

OR

255 J. LEMON

vv. 5 and 10

256 H. SMART

Alternative chant for verses 24 to 30:

257 S. ARNOLD

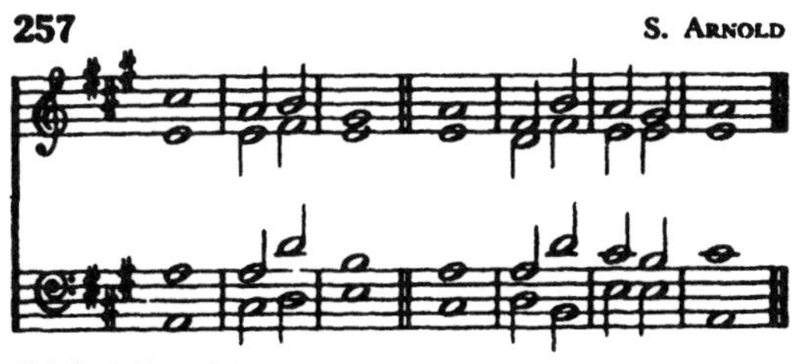

Original Key: B♭

OR

258 J. L. HOPKINS

Original Key: D

Alternative chant for verses 24 to 30:

259 J. STAINER

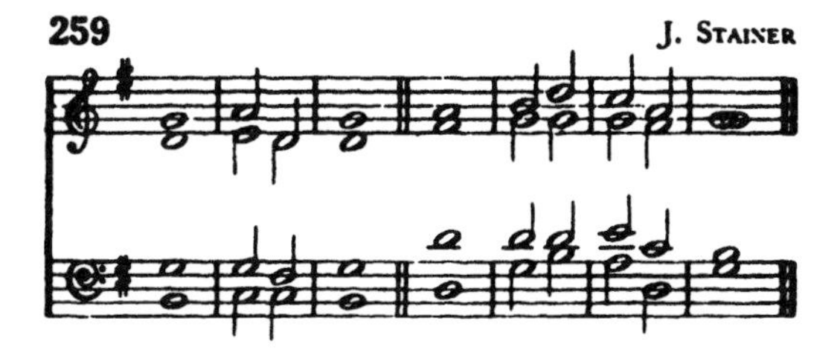

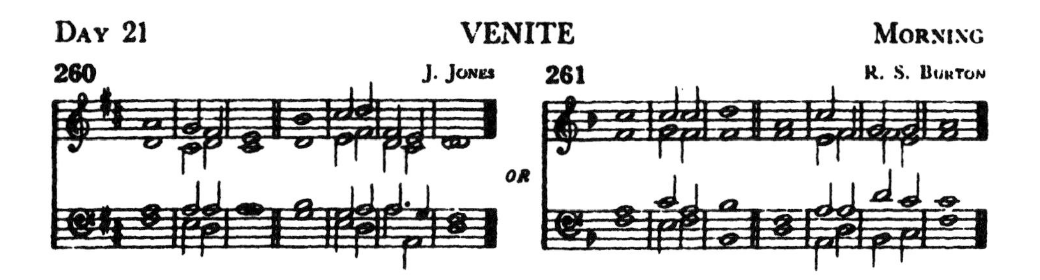

PSALM 105

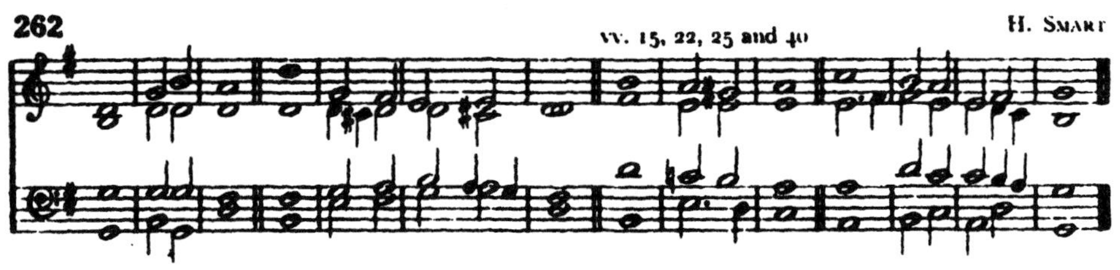

Original Key: A

Alternative chant for verses 23 to 35:

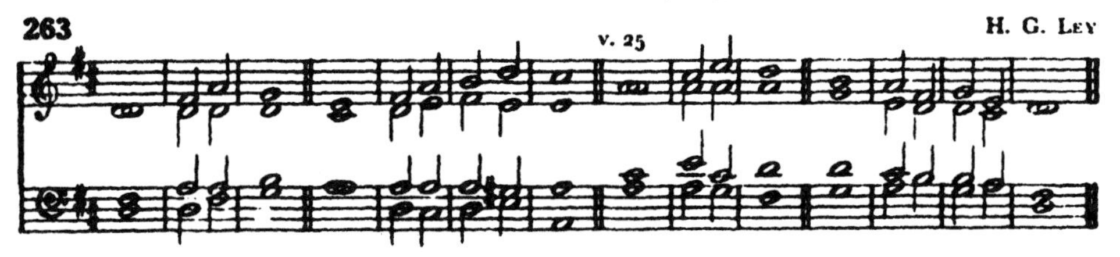

OR

Original Key: D

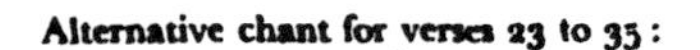
Alternative chant for verses 23 to 35:

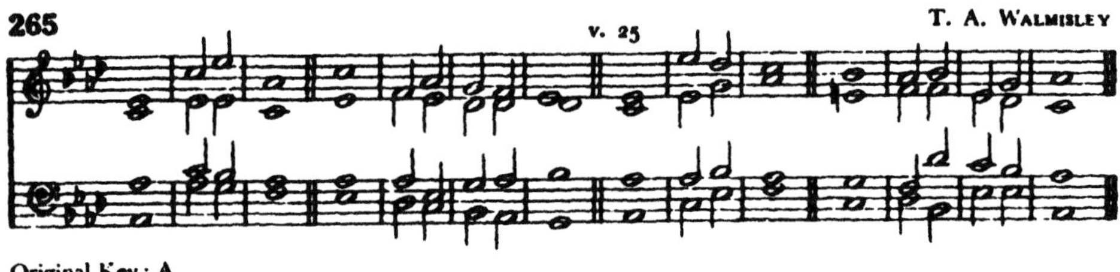

Original Key: A

verses 1 to 5, 8 to 12, 30 and 31 and 43 to end

Verse 46 may be sung in Unison.

verses 6 and 7, 13 to 29 and 32 to 42

Also suitable: Chants 188 and 187, 196 and 197, and 220 and 222.

Alternative chant for the Doxology (verse 46):

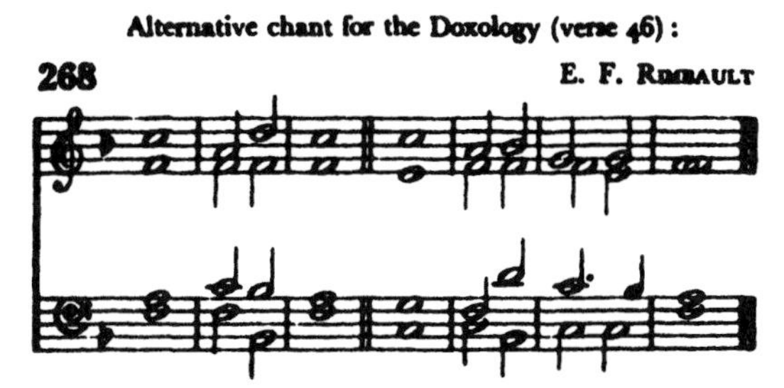

(If this chant is used, verse 45 must be sung to the second half of Chant 266.)

269 F. A. G. Ouseley

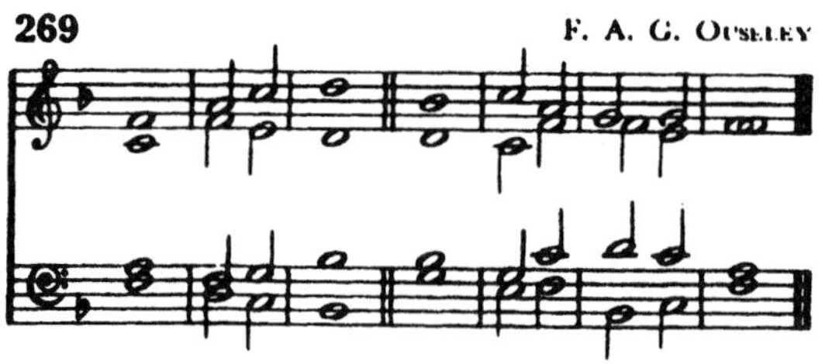

Original Key: G

PSALM 107

verses 1 to 3, 8 and 9, 15 and 16, 21 and 22 and 31 to end

270 (S) G. J. Elvey

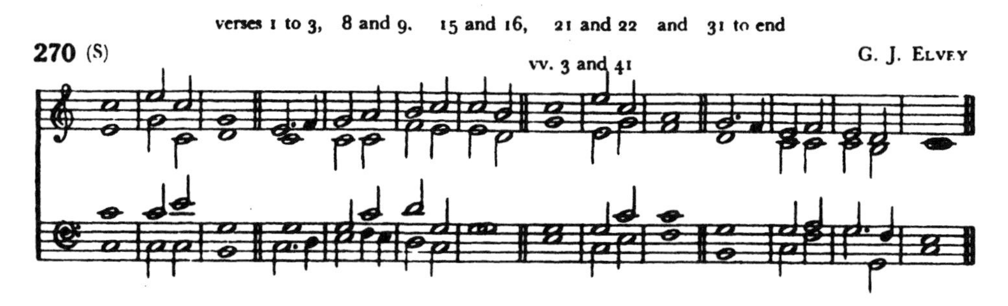

OR

verses 1 to 3, 8 and 9, 15 and 16, 21 and 22 and 31 to end

271 (S) H. G. Ley

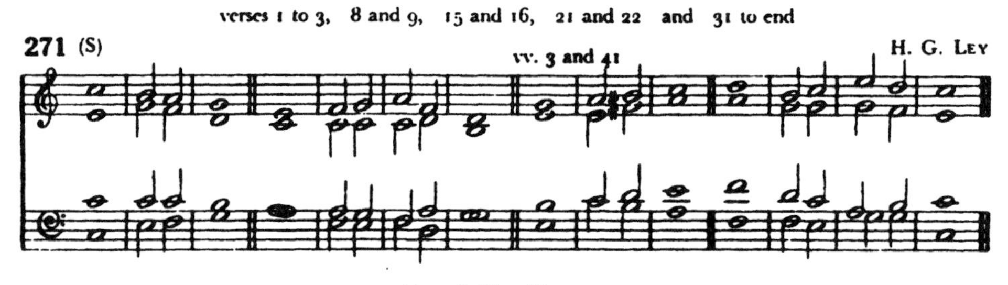

Also suitable: Chant 199

verses 4 to 7, 10 to 14, 17 to 20 and 23 to 30

272 J. Battishill

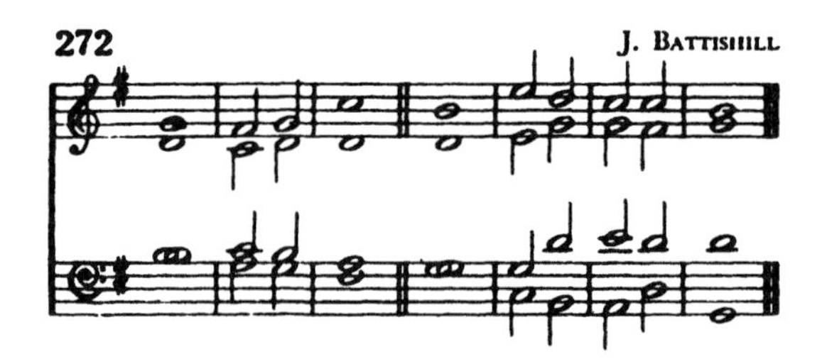

PSALM 108

verses 1 to 5

273 ANONYMOUS

Verse 5 may be sung in Unison.

verse 6 to end

274 F. A. G. OUSELEY

PSALM 109

verses 1 to 28

275 vv. 19 and 24 H. SMART

verse 29 to end

276 C. F. SOUTH

VENITE

277 STEPHENS

278 D. B. EPERSON

Original Key: B♭

PSALM 110

279 T. A. WALMISLEY

280 H. SMART

Original Key: D

PSALM 111

281 R. MASSEY

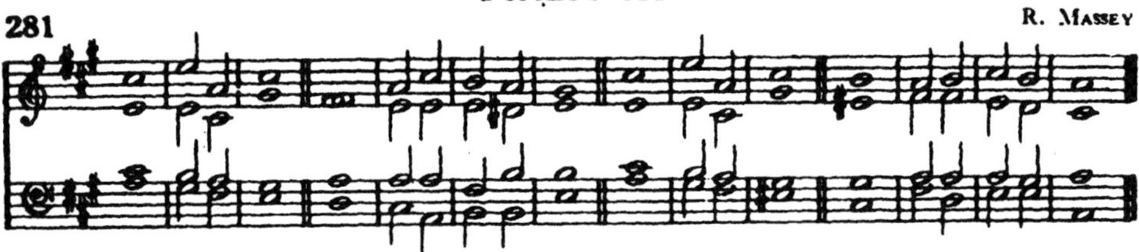

OR

282 J. RANDALL

PSALM 112

283 E. BLAKE

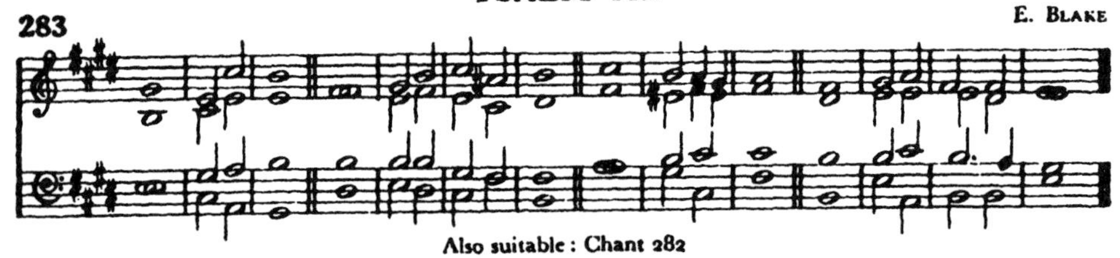

Also suitable: Chant 282

PSALM 113

284 J. TURLE

OR

285 W. DYCE

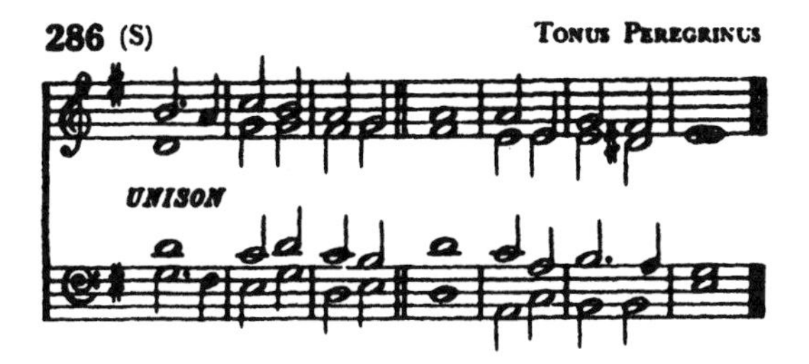
286 (S)
TONUS PEREGRINUS
UNISON

PSALM 115

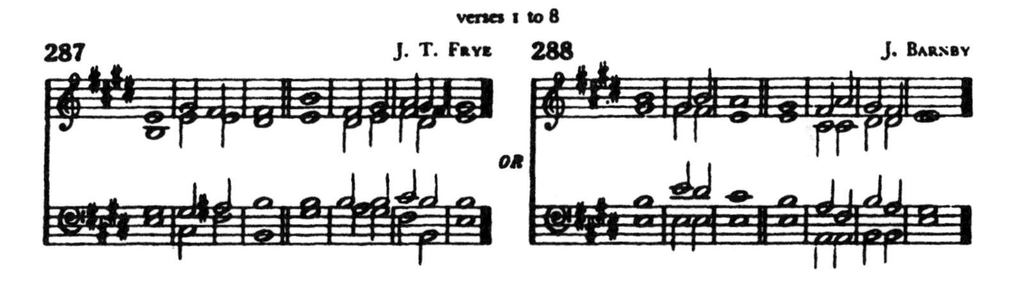
verses 1 to 8
287
J. T. FRYE
OR
288
J. BARNBY

verse 9 to end
289
J. GOSS

290 F. A. G. OUSELEY — 291 H. SMART

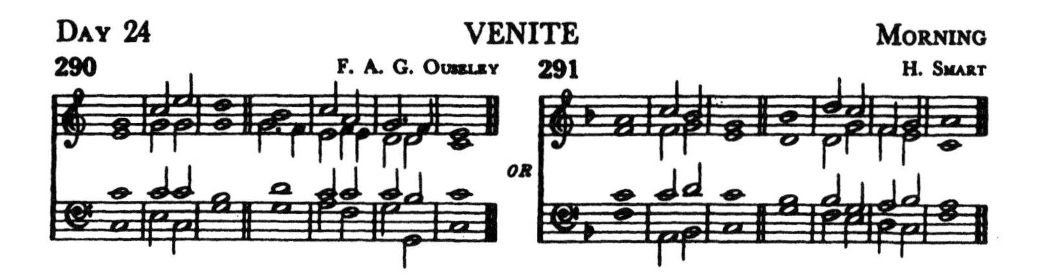

PSALM 116

292 H. ALDRICH

PSALM 117

293 J. TURLE — 294 C. H. MOODY

PSALM 118

verses 1 to 4 and 19 to end

295 R. GOODSON

Verses 1 and 29 may be sung in Unison.

verses 5 to 18

296 E. J. HOPKINS

vv. 7 and 12

Also suitable (for the whole Psalm): Chant 386

verses 1 to 8

297 R. WOODWARD

Original Key: A

verses 9 to 16

298 K. J. PYE

verses 17 to 24

299 T. S. DUPUIS

Original Key: A

verses 25 to 32

300 J. GOSS

VENITE

301 T. W. HANFORTH — OR — **302** F. H. CHAMPNEYS

Original Key: G

PSALM 119

verses 33 to 40

303 S. ELVEY

verses 41 to 48

304 H. W. RHODES

verses 49 to 56

305 G. J. ELVEY

verses 57 to 64

306 P. ARMES

verses 65 to 72

307 S. MARCHANT

verses 73 to 80

308 G. J. Elvey

verses 81 to 88

309 S. Elvey

verses 89 to 96

310 C. E. Miller

verses 97 to 104

311 G. J. Elvey

312 W. RUSSELL

313 M. GREENE

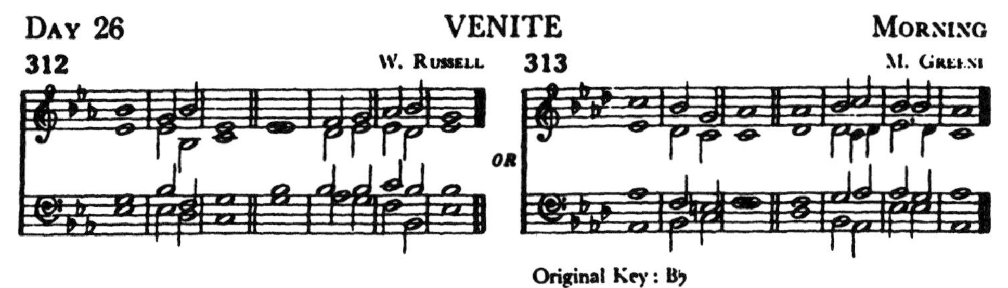

Original Key: B♭

PSALM 119

verses 105 to 112

314 J. LEMON

verses 113 to 120

315 W. RUSSELL

Original Key: E

verses 121 to 128

316 THE EARL OF MORNINGTON

Original Key: D

verses 129 to 136

317 J. GOSS

Original Key: A

verses 137 to 144

318 T. A. WALMISLEY

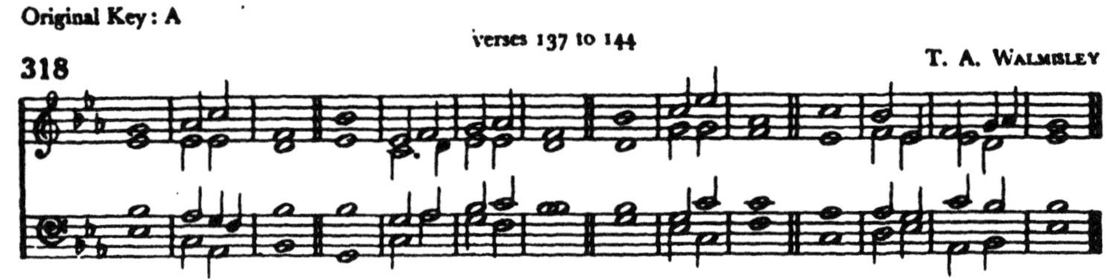

verses 145 to 152

319 G. HEATHCOTE

Original Key: A

OR

verses 145 to 152

320 T. ATTWOOD

Original Key: A♭

verses 153 to 160

321 E. HIGGINS

Original Key: F

verses 161 to 168

322 E. J. HOPKINS

verse 169 to end

323 E. HODGSON (and Others)

324 H. G. LEY

325 T. A. WALMISLEY

PSALM 120

326 E. F. RIMBAULT

327 WALFORD DAVIES

Original Key: B minor

PSALM 121

328 (S) H. G. LEY

OR

329 (S) J. TURLE

Original Key: A

PSALM 122

330 G. M. GARRETT

OR

331 J. STAINER (from BEETHOVEN)

Also suitable: Chant 56

PSALM 123

PSALM 124

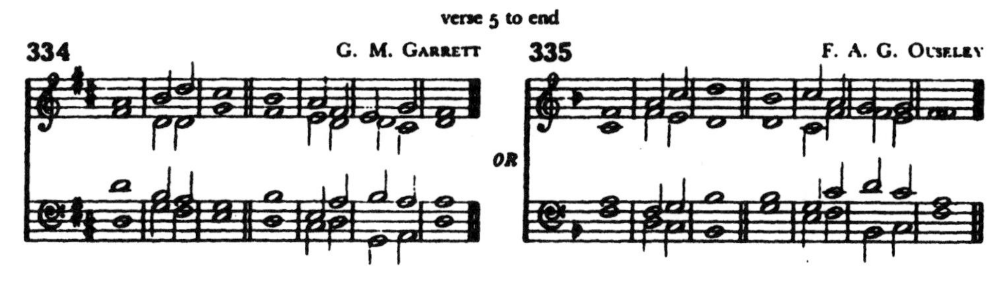

Original Key: G

PSALM 125

336 G. J. Elvey

VENITE

(For use when one or more of these Evening Psalms is sung as a Proper Psalm at Matins.)

Day 27 PSALM 126 Evening

Also suitable: Chant 183

PSALM 127

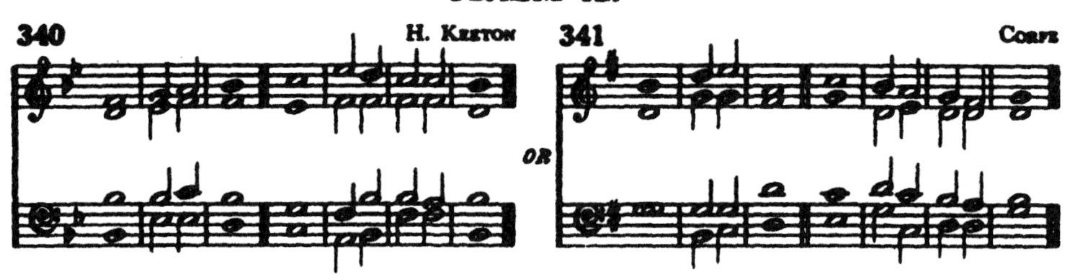

PSALM 128

PSALM 129

343 G. C. Martin

OR

344 J. L. Rogers

Also suitable: Chants 28 and 194

PSALM 130

345 J. Turle (from H. Purcell)

OR

346 (S) C. Hylton Stewart

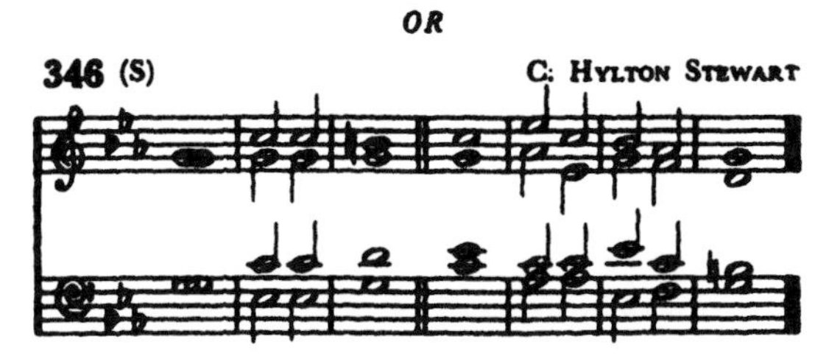

Also suitable: Chants 147 and 369

PSALM 131

347 D. B. Eperson *OR* **348** M. M. Bridges

Also suitable: Chant 49

VENITE

349 — R. Goodson

350 — J. Goss

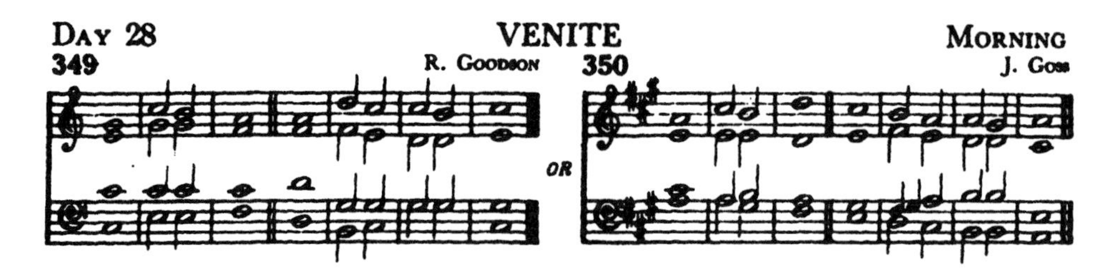

PSALM 132

351 — verses 1 to 10 — R. Farrant

352 — verse 11 to end — J. L. Hopkins

PSALM 133

353 — E. Elgar

354 — G. F. Cobb

Original Key: G

PSALM 134

355 — F. A. G. Ouseley

356 — J. Battishill

Original Key: A

PSALM 135

357 — vv. 7, 12 and 21 — J. Stafford Smith

OR

358 — vv. 7, 12 and 21 — H. Smart

359 (S) — vv. 3, 12 and 25 — C. H. LLOYD

Original Key: B♭

OR

360 (TRIPLE CHANT) — H. M. HAVERGAL

(Verses 19 and 20, 21 and 22, 26 and 27, and the Gloria, must be sung as couplets, by omitting the portion of the chant indicated above.)

PSALM 137

361 — W. R. BEXFIELD OR **362** (S) — C. H. LLOYD

Original Key: C♯ minor

OR

363 — T. TALLIS

PSALM 138

364 — L. L. DIX OR **365** — REGINALD A. ATKINS

VENITE

366 G. J. ELVEY — 367 E. G. MONK

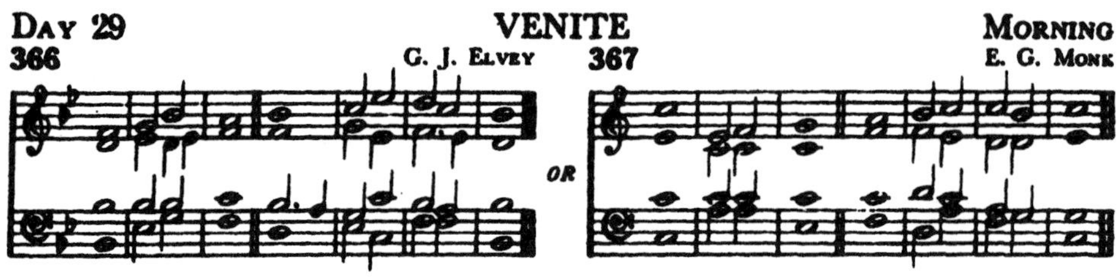

Original Key: D

PSALM 139

368 — W. BAYLEY

vv. 5 and 16

Also suitable: Chant 100

PSALM 140

369* — W. E. SMITH

v. 3

Original Key: C♯ minor

OR

370 — R. CLARK

v. 3

PSALM 141

371 — H. W. RHODES

v. 11

OR

372 — F. A. G. OUSELEY

v. 11

*Originally composed for Psalm 130

373 — J. BLOW

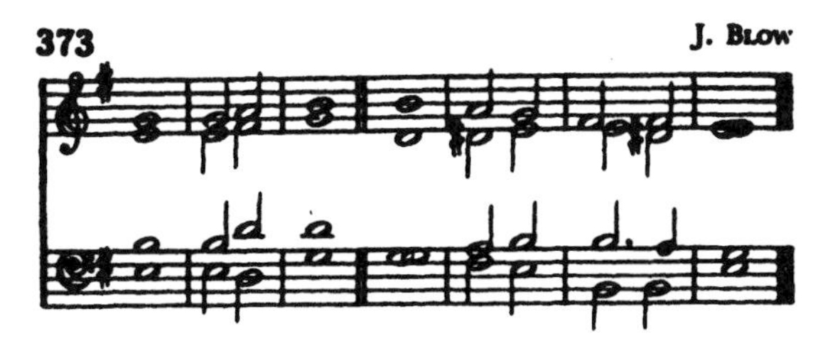

374 — C. A. WICKES

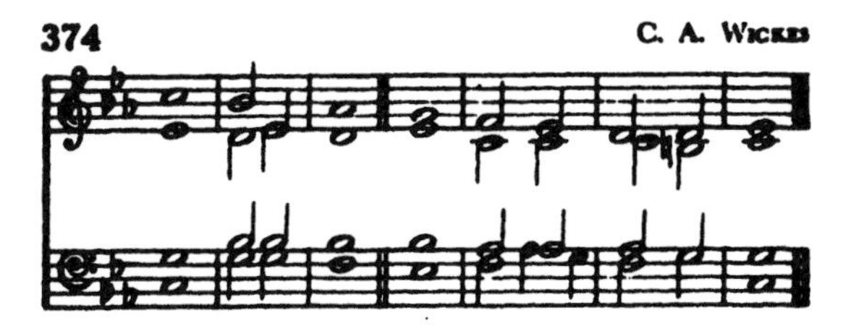

Original Key : D minor

375 (S) — M. M. BRIDGES

OR

376 (S) — J. TURLE (from J. S. BACH)

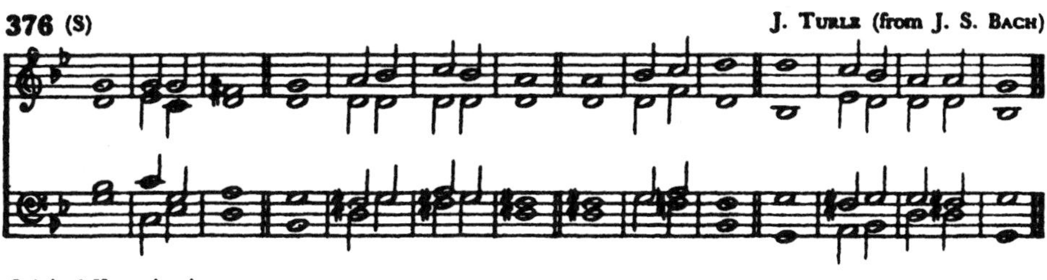

Original Key : A minor

Also suitable : Chant 368

PSALM 144

PSALM 145

PSALM 146

*The third and fourth quarters of this chant are identical with the first and second quarters, respectively, but with the chords in the reverse order.

OR

Also suitable: Chant 130

Also suitable: Chants 96, 255 and 387

PSALM 149

OR

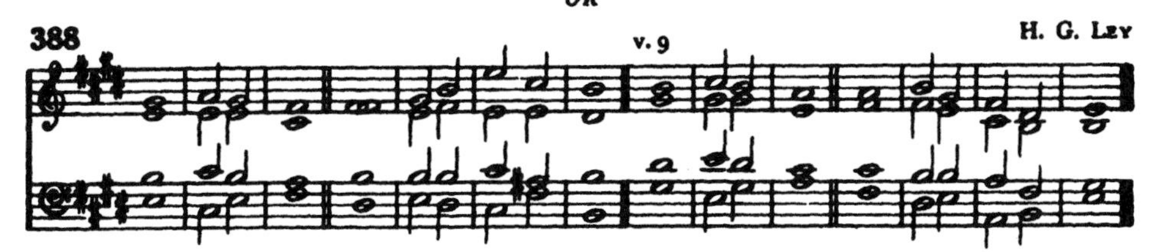

OR

The Chant Setting on the next two pages

PSALM 150

390 (S) C. V. STANFORD

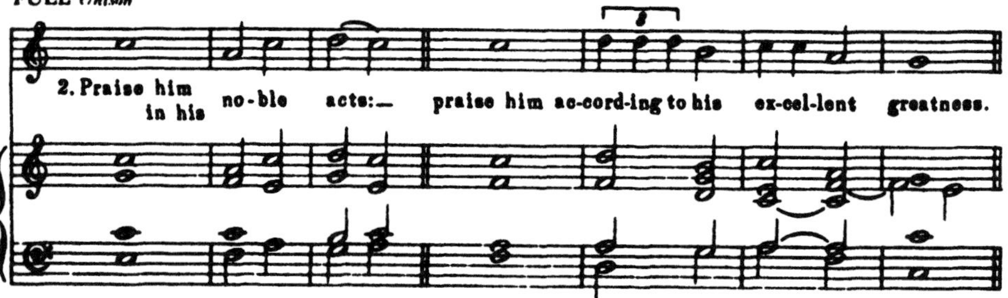

FULL
ff
6. Let every thing that hath breath: praise the Lord.
ff
ff

FULL
Glory be to the Father, and to the Son: and to the Holy Ghost;

As it was in the beginning, is now and ever shall be: world without end. A - - men.

PSALM 150

Revised Psalter Version

C.V. Stanford

By permission of the Registrars of the Convocations of Canterbury and York

FULL
ff
6. Let everything that hath breath praise the Lord: O praise ye the Lord.
ff
ff

FULL
Glory be to the Father, and to the Son: and to the Ho-ly Ghost;

As it was in the beginning, is now and ev-er shall be: world without end. A - - men.

ANTHEMS FOR MIXED VOICES

ASTON, Peter (b. 1938)
ALLELUYA PSALLAT

BAIRSTOW, Edward C (1874-1946)
SAVE US, O LORD
SING YE TO THE LORD

BARRELL, Bernard (b. 1919)
TWO SHORT ANTHEMS

BENSON, John S
A LYDIAN INTROIT

BURRELL, Diana (b. 1948)
TWO BLESSINGS

CAMPBELL, Sidney
SING WE MERRILY UNTO GOD OUR STRENGTH

DALBY, Martin (b. 1942)
AD FLUMINA BABYLONIAE
MATER SALUTARIS

DERING, Richard (c. 1580-1630)
AVE MARIA

DYSON, George (1883-1964)
CONFORTARE

ECCARD, Johann (1553-1611)
PRESENTATION OF CHRIST IN THE TEMPLE

GARDINER, H Balfour (1877-1950)
EVENING HYMN (TE LUCIS ANTE TERMINUM)

GIBBONS, Orlando (1583-1625)
THIS IS THE RECORD OF JOHN

GREENE, Maurice (1696-1755)
THOU VISITEST THE EARTH (H)

HARRIS, William H (1883-1973)
COME DOWN, O LOVE DIVINE

HARVEY, Jonathan (b. 1939)
THE DOVE DESCENDING
I LOVE THE LORD

HOWELLS, Herbert (1892-1983)
REGINA CAELI
SALVE REGINA AND O SALUTARIS HOSTIA

HYDE, Derek
A PSALM OF CELEBRATION

IVES, Grayston
LET ALL THE WORLD IN EVERY CORNER SING

JEFFREYS, George (c. 1610-1685)
A MUSIC STRANGE
WHISPER IT EASILY

JOUBERT, John (b. 1927)
GLORY AND HONOUR

LEIGHTON, Kenneth (1929-1988)
THE BEAUTY OF HOLINESS
WHAT LOVE IS THIS OF THINE?

LEWIS, Jeffrey
HYMNUS ANTE SOMNUM

LLOYD WEBBER, Andrew (b. 1948)
PIE JESU

McCABE, John (b. 1939)
MOTET

MILNER, Anthony (b. 1925)
FESTIVAL CHANT

OLIVER, Stephen (b. 1950)
THIS IS THE VOICE

arr PAGET, Michael
AIN'T THAT GOOD NEWS

PURCELL, Henry (1659-1695)
HEAR MY PRAYER, O LORD
MY BELOVED SPAKE
O SING UNTO THE LORD A NEW SONG

ROSE, Gregory
VESPERS FOR MARY MAGDALEN

SAMPSON, Godfrey (1902-1949)
COME, MY WAY, MY TRUTH, MY LIFE!

SHAVE, Eric
HUMBLE ACCESS

SPICER, Paul (b. 1952)
COME OUT LAZAR (COME OUT, LAZARUS)

STANFORD, Charles Villiers (1852-1924)
HOW BEAUTEOUS ARE THEIR FEET
O PRAISE GOD IN HIS HOLINESS (PSALM 150)

SUMSION, Herbert (b. 1899)
FEAR NOT, O LAND

TRAVERS, John (c. 1703-1758)
ASCRIBE UNTO THE LORD

WALKER, Robert (b. 1946)
HERE, O MY LORD, I SEE THEE FACE TO FACE
O LORD, THOU HAST SEARCHED ME OUT
THOU WILT KEEP HIM IN PERFECT PEACE

WEIR, Judith (b. 1954)
ASCENDING INTO HEAVEN

WESLEY, Samuel (1766-1837)
IN EXITU ISRAEL

WESLEY, Samuel Sebastian (1810-1876)
BLESSED BE THE GOD AND FATHER
THOU WILT KEEP HIM IN PERFECT PEACE
THE WILDERNESS

WILLS, Arthur (b. 1926)
I HUNGER AND I THURST

CANTICLE SETTINGS FOR EVENING PRAYER

MAGNIFICAT & NUNC DIMITTIS

ARNOLD, Samuel
In A

AYLEWARD, Richard
SHORT EVENING SERVICE

BAIRSTOW, Edward
In D

BALL, Michael
MANCHESTER SERVICE

BLOW, John
In F

BREWER, Herbert
In E flat

DYSON, George
In F

HAWES, Jack
In D

HOLST, Gustav
NUNC DIMITTIS ONLY

HOWELLS, Herbert
CHICESTER CATHEDRAL
COLLEGIUM REGALE
GLOUCESTER CATHEDRAL
ST AUGUSTINE'S, BIRMINGHAM
ST JOHN'S COLLEGE, CAMBRIDGE
ST PAUL'S CATHEDRAL
ST PETER'S, WESTMINSTER
WINCHESTER CATHEDRAL
WORCESTER CATHEDRAL
YORK MINSTER

IRELAND, John
In F

JACKSON, Francis
HEREFORD CATHEDRAL

JOUBERT, John
In C

KELLY, Bryan
EMMANUEL

LEIGHTON, Kenneth
COLLEGIUM MAGDALENAE OXONIENESE

LLOYD, Richard
HEREFORD CATHEDRAL

McCABE, John
SALISBURY

STANFORD, Charles
In B flat
n A

SUMSION, Herbert
In G

SWAYNE, Giles
MAGNIFICAT ONLY

WALMISLEY, Thomas
In D minor

WALKER, Robert
PETERBOROUGH CATHEDRAL

WOOD, Charles
In D
in E flat